JOHN C. FRÉMONT
From a steel engraving made in 1856
at the time of his presidential campaign.
From the author's collection.

THE FRÉMONT CANNON
HIGH UP AND FAR BACK

*Unravelling the puzzle of the
brass cannon abandoned in 1844
and never recovered from
California's Sierra Nevada*

by
ERNEST ALLEN LEWIS

Revised Second Edition

WESTERN TRAILS PRESS
18014 Jayhawk Drive
Penn Valley, CA   95946-9206

Dedication

*To all the courageous men
who explored and opened the American West.*

LIBRARY OF CONGRESS CATALOG CARD NUMBER 92-60710
ISBN 0-9633604-1-8

CONTENTS

ACKNOWLEDGEMENT 6

INTRODUCTION...11

I   IN SEARCH OF A DESTINY...15

II   THE SECOND EXPEDITION – ACROSS SOUTH PASS...23

III   FROM FORT HALL TO SATAN'S PLAYGROUND – THE GREAT BASIN.........................37

IV   THE CANNON IS ABANDONED...45

V   THE NEVADA MUSEUM CANNON...57

VI   WASHOE INDIANS VERSUS A FRENCH HOWITZER 71

VII THE FRÉMONT- KEARNY CANNON...79

VIII A LOST CANNON IN SEARCH OF A FINDER...83

ADVICE AND COUNSEL..86

BIBLIOGRAPHY...87

FINANCIAL RECORDS - FRÉMONT'S 2ND EXPEDITION

MILEAGE RECORDS - FRÉMONT'S 2ND EXPEDITION

LATITUDE AND LONGITUDE OF FRÉMONT'S 2ND EXPEDITION

ILLUSTRATIONS

PORTRAIT OF JOHN C. FRÉMONT ....*Frontispiece*

MAP OF FRÉMONT'S ROUTE IN THE BRIDGEPORT AREA 9

Harper's Weekly - Maj. Gen. JOHN C. FRÉMONT - 1861 REVIEWING TROOPS 10

Harper's Weekly - Maj. Gen. JOHN C. FRÉMONT - 1861 IN PRAIRIE COSTUME 13

COL. KIT CARSON - 1864...36

CELILO FALLS, THE DALLES AND FORT VANCOUVER - 1845..44

SITE OF FRÉMONT'S CAMP AT BRIDGEPORT 47

DEVIL'S GATE...47

BURCHAM FLAT 48

SOUTH FACE OF MOUNTAIN 8422 48

SADDLE OF MOUNTAIN 8422 49

NORTH FACE OF MOUNTAIN 8422 49

PREUSS' MAP OF THE ROUTE...50

THE HAWKINS DERINGER 55

FRÉMONT IN THE 1840s...65

CHARLES PREUSS 65

PYRAMID LAKE AS SKETCHED BY PREUSS...66

PYRAMID LAKE TODAY..67

THE NEVADA MUSEUM CANNON 67

THE NEVADA MUSEUM CANNON IN 1896 68

THE FORT CHURCHILL CANNON - 1884 69

MOUNTAIN HOWITZER AMMO, RANGES AND WEIGHTS...70

THE CYRUS - ALGER CANNON PACKED ON HORSEBACK...75

THE HORSESHOE CLIFF ON MOUNTAIN 8422, TWO VIEWS 76

HARRY TOM, "CHIEF WHITE WING"...77

PORTRAIT OF JOHN C. FRÉMONT AT 77 YEARS 78

Unless otherwise credited in captions, the illustrations are from the author's photographs.

ACKNOWLEDGMENT

This book would not and could not have been written without the encouragement and skilled assistance of Carl Briggs, an outstanding historian, writer and former editor of Scripps League Newspapers. The author is deeply in his debt.

Close friend and historian, Marshall A. Fey was greatly instrumental in the design and production of the second and third editions of this book. His knowledge, talent and hard work were invaluable. (1992)

Without the gracious aid and cooperation of the State of Nevada Museum at Carson City, Nevada, an accurate and detailed study of the Frémont Cannon would be an impossibility. The Frémont files they have compiled over the past forty-seven years are a treasure-trove for the interested researcher. Also, the Nevada Historical Society, Reno, Nevada, was most helpful in making available their research facilities and did everything possible to aid in the quest for needed materials.

To my daughters, Barbara E. Jacobsen and Christine M. Lewis for their typing of the manuscript, and many other friends who gave encouragement and advice along the way, I give my sincere thanks. No writer ever does his job entirely alone.

ERNEST ALLEN LEWIS

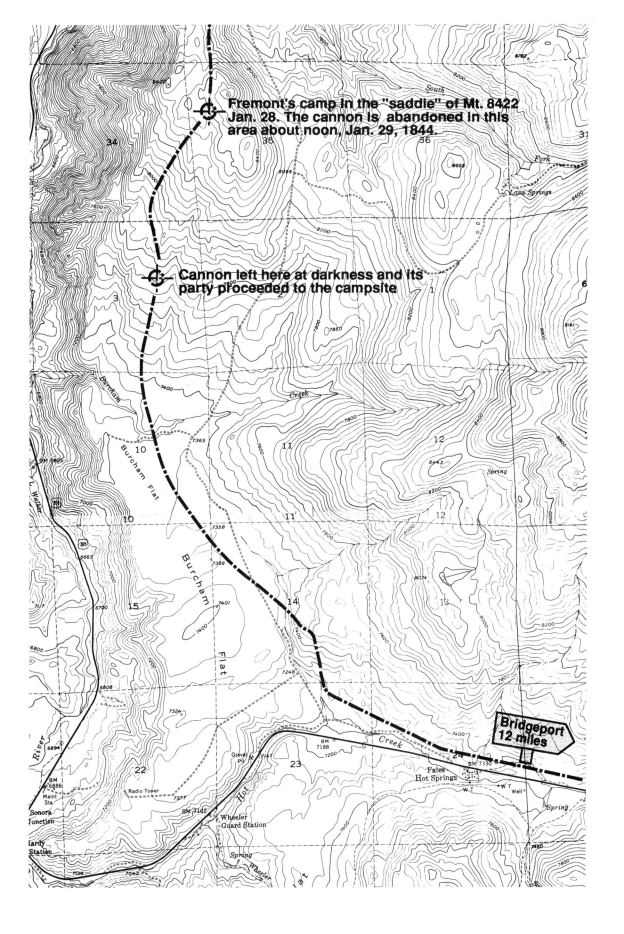

Major General John C. Frémont 1861 Reviewing Troops
Harper's Weekly - October 12th 1861

Lake Wildwood, California
August 23, 1979

INTRODUCTION

If John C. Frémont was a child of destiny he was also fated to be her bastard. His keen intellect, indomitable courage and unique physical stamina carried him to the brink of legendary greatness,but his impetuousness, aggressive ambition and ill-tempered indiscretions ultimately removed him from the scenes of political, military and financial power he desperately sought. Still, what he did accomplish so far outweighs his failures that his critics are reduced to silly babblings as they direct their diatribes and abusive invectives at his human failings. This is to be expected when any public figure occasionally fails, whether that failure is his fault or not. Jealous literary crocodiles are always present to criticize persons more capable and successful than they.

Frémont's career was a spectacular series of peaks and valleys. He married one of the most beautiful and talented women of his time, Jessie Anne Benton, the daughter of Senator Thomas Hart Benton, who for thirty years was one of the most powerful public figures in Washington. Frémont deservedly achieved early fame as a scientific explorer and reporter of the American West. The publication of his reports and maps in 1845 were almost as responsible as the discovery of California gold for the mass human migration from east to west that subsequently took place. His fame and popularity were further enhanced in California when on his third expedition he played a prominent and perhaps decisive role in the California Rebellion. At the peak of his popularity, though, his world came crashing down when he refused to obey the orders of General Stephen Watts Kearny and was subsequently court martialed. Found guilty after a long and highly publicized trial, he received a slap on the wrist and could have remained in the army, but his pride made him resign. Fortune once again smiled on him when he returned to California and almost by accident purchased the Mariposa land grant. Within months he was a very wealthy man as gold was dug out of his mines in enormous amounts. Back in the limelight and among old friends and associates, he was elected California's first senator. After serving a shortened term, he lost the next election on the 144th ballot because of his anti-slavery position. A few years later in 1856, he was the Republican Party's first presidential candidate. Although defeated by Buchanan, his liberal anti-slavery and free soil platform paved the way for Lincoln's election in 1860. As a Major General in the Union Army and in command of the Western Department at St. Louis, Missouri, he issued the first slavery emancipation proclamation in October 1861. At the insistence of powerful political enemies who accused Frémont of ineffective leadership and corruption, President Lincoln removed him from his command when Frémont refused to rescind the proclamation. Ironically, history will forever deify Lincoln as the deliverer of America's people in bondage, although it would be another two years before he would issue his effective proclamation, and then only to those states in rebellion against the Union. In the ensuing years Frémont's financial empire collapsed when he made poor railroad investments, and crooked lawyers and land grabbers stole his ranch. His term as Governor of Arizona Territory was his last official position. He died in New York City, July 13, 1890, a few days after Congress voted to award him the pension of a Major

General. Cities, counties, streets, valleys, mountains and lakes are named for him. Perhaps these are sufficient monuments.

The first three chapters of this book possibly will be boring to Frémont scholars, although there are some observations they may find interesting. These chapters deal with his early life and the influences and circumstances that led to his explorations, together with an edited review of his report on the second expedition. These chapters are included as there must be a foundation for any investigation into the history of the little cannon he abandoned on his second expedition to Oregon and California in 1843 and 1844 and a short simple summary of his early years seemed to be the most logical place to start. Since there are far more treasure seekers and students of western history than there are Frémont scholars, they can use the early chapters as a review of this fascinating era of experimentation, political instability and geographical ambition and, Frémont's place in this cauldron.

This book is not intended to spotlight John C. Frémont, although he obviously plays a prominent role. His outstanding biographers, Allan Nevins and Ferol Egan, have done exceptional jobs in telling the story of his very eventful life. Frémont, Kit Carson, Tom Fitzpatrick, Charles Preuss and many others will make their contributions in the following pages, but this story is about the twelve-pound howitzer Frémont abandoned when his exhausted men and animals could carry it no further against the awesome granite walls of the eastern Sierra Nevada and its bitterly cold storm-swept midwinter snowdrifts.

For over one hundred years Frémont's cannon was thought to have been found. This is probably the single most important circumstance that has kept it in its mountain hiding place. When Frémont requisitioned and took the cannon on what was supposedly a purely scientific expedition, he stirred up a political hornet's nest that almost stopped the venture before it started. At the time of its loss the little howitzer caused considerable controversy, but was soon forgotten as monumental events shoved it aside. The California Rebellion, the Mexican War, the California gold rush, the Civil War, the transcontinental railroad and a sea of humanity moving west removed the importance of one small howitzer from the minds of politicians, military men and historians. It wasn't until the 1940's that serious questions started to arise concerning Frémont's lost cannon.

My interest in the howitzer began in 1957 while visiting friends in Bridgeport, California. They could hardly wait for the coming weekend so they could go cannon hunting. My interest was piqued when they related a number of local legends concerning cannon sightings. Admittedly, they had no evidence to rely on other than the campfire stories of hunters and fishermen, but the sheer numbers of the sightings were enough to convince them that somewhere in the mountains within thirty miles of Bridgeport there was a cannon, its wooden wheels crumbling with age, its irons rusting, but with its brass barrel intact and awaiting a lucky finder. I accompanied them on their trek into the wilderness. The mountains, valleys and streams were spectacular, the air exhilarating, and the treasure search mind-boggling. Suddenly I found myself believing that the cannon was in the next grove of trees, or around the next bend or in the next canyon. The day was so spiritually uplifting it didn't matter when I found later we were forty miles from where the cannon was probably located.

In the ensuing years I followed many twisting paths, obtaining and assimilating as much information as possible from libraries and bookstores throughout the west, interviewing people who supposedly had seen the cannon or knew someone who had seen it, and of course walking hundreds of miles over an awesome part of nature's gift to California and Nevada - the Sierra Nevada. Through the years very few people have actively or seriously searched for Frémont's cannon. As a matter of fact I've never encountered another searcher in the area since my Bridgeport friends passed away. Only those few friends and family members I've taken to "the mountain" know where my research has led.

As the years passed, so passed my physical ability to climb mountains, and my secrets and personal ego don't seem to be as important as they once were. Most importantly I want Frémont's lost howitzer to be found. Other than Sir Francis Drake's "Ye Platte of Brass," it is one of the last unfound artifacts of the early western history of the United States. Its historical significance is unquestioned. In this book you will follow what I believe to be a reasonably well-researched trail to the location where Frémont abandoned the cannon. I'm convinced the evidence is overwhelming that it is still there or within a mile or two of that place. I'm sure you'll enjoy your walk … high up and far back.

Maj. Gen. John C. Frémont in his Prairie Costume
Harper's Weekly-July 13th 1861

Chapter I

IN SEARCH OF A DESTINY

SOMEWHERE east of the Sierra summit in the tumbled volcanic canyons of the California-Nevada border country lies the wreckage of a U.S. Army brass cannon. Engendered in an era of military innocence, steeped in political controversy, and immortalized in popular legend, the little howitzer has been the object of speculation and intensive search for more than 145 years. The cannon is still there, somewhere in the craggy mountains bordering the West Walker River, right where John C. Frémont abandoned it on January 29, 1844.

JESSIE FRÉMONT wrote to her husband that he must not ask why, but must start at once, ready or not ready. His animals could rest and fatten at Bent's Fort. Only go — now! *(Mrs. Frémont gave two different accounts of how this message was sent to her husband. In the "Memoirs" manuscript she said it was sent by one of the Derosier brothers; in the* Century *magazine article she states it was sent by Basil Lajeunesse. It may or may not have occurred, she had a vivid imagination.)*

Second Lieutenant John Frémont, Topographical Engineers of the U.S. Army, engaged in completing his outfit in preparation for his second expedition to the Rocky Mountains and on to Oregon, realized immediately the urgency in his wife's hurriedly written note. It was May 29, 1843 and he had been organizing the expedition at Kaw Landing (Kansas City, Missouri) for three weeks, but trusting his loyal and dedicated wife implicitly, he departed hastily in a rainstorm and camped on the muddy prairie four miles from the settlement. He was not to know the reason until more than fourteen months later when he returned from this most successful scientific exploration.

The reason for leaving so hurriedly was "the cannon." Early in the second week of May 1843, Frémont had requisitioned a brass twelve-pound mountain howitzer from the Army arsenal at St. Louis. Heavy weapon designations were different in Frémont's time than they are today. A cannon's poundage size meant the weight of the projectile and its powder charge. Normally a twelve-pound howitzer fired a ten to ten and a half-pound shell or canister and was propelled by a two pound charge — thus a twelve-pound cannon.

Captain William H. Bell, commanding the arsenal, questioned the requisition and the necessity for such a piece of military ordnance for what was supposed to be a scientific expedition. However, as the congressional record shows, Colonel Stephen Watts Kearny, Commander of the Third Military Department with Headquarters at Jefferson Barracks, near St. Louis, approved the request. The little brass howitzer became an immediate topic of controversy in Washington, D.C. and St. Louis. Col. Kearny was criticized for allowing Frémont to requisition the howitzer, but at the time, Kearny had more important problems on his hands. His dragoons and infantry were engaged in several forays, skirmishes and major expeditions along the Santa Fe Trail. Indians were attacking, killing and robbing traders, and Texans and Mexicans were engaged in numerous border shooting incidents.

Captain Bell sent a letter to his superiors in Washington complaining about the entire howitzer episode. In true bureaucratic fashion, he didn't like the situation because the request had not gone through the proper channels. This letter was forwarded to James M.

Porter, acting Secretary of War, who brought it to the attention of Colonel J. Abert, Commander of the Topographical Engineers. On May 22, 1843 Abert dispatched a letter to Frémont scolding him for requisitioning the howitzer and questioning its use on a peaceful expedition to gather scientific knowledge. He ordered Frémont to report back to Washington immediately. It was this letter that Jessie Frémont intercepted. And, but for Jessie's timely intervention, in all probability it would have brought the expedition to a standstill before it got started. More importantly, at least for this work, the little cannon did accompany the expedition. It left its wheel marks across nearly 3900 miles of prairies, mountains and deserts. When it could go no further because of the deep snows of the California Sierra Nevada and exhausted condition of the men and animals, it was abandoned above the West Walker River in the Sweetwater Mountains approximately seventeen miles northwest of present-day Bridgeport, California. Its odyssey was heroic, its uses few.

John C. Frémont was born in controversy and scandal January 21, 1813. He was an illegitimate child and that shadow was to follow him throughout his life, especially in his presidential campaign of 1856. His father was Charles Frémont, a Frenchman probably from Lyons, France, who had made his way to Virginia by way of Santo Domingo, or perhaps the West Indies. He may have been a fugitive or refugee of the turmoil caused by the French Revolution. Frémont left France about 1800 and spent the next seven or eight years as a captive of the British, but apparently with a great deal of freedom. Prisoners not considered dangerous were allowed to pursue their normal occupations, thus for the most part supporting themselves and saving the authorities considerable money. This was a commonly used penal system at the time. It is known that Frémont supplemented his prisoner's allowance by making basketware, doing cabinet work, and painting ceiling frescoes. If not an artist, he was at least dexterous with his hands.

When Frémont arrived in Virginia, isn't exactly known, but by the spring of 1808 he was teaching French at a fashionable academy directed by L. H. Girardin and David Doyle, near Richmond. He rented a house from Major John Pryor, a veteran officer of the American Revolution in his mid-seventies, though still quite vigorous. It was in this situation that he met Ann Beverly Whiting Pryor, the Major's twenty-eight-year-old wife, who was to become the mother of John Charles Frémont.

Ann Whiting was the spirited youngest daughter of Col. Thomas Whiting, a wealthy land owner in Glouchester County, Virginia, and a leader in the Virginia House of Burgesses. After Col. Whiting died, Ann's mother married a man named Carey, who subsequently and rather quickly spent most of her estate, leaving her in poor financial condition. Ann was raised by an older sister and in 1796 at the tender age of seventeen, she was married to John Pryor, sixty-two. Whether this was a marriage of love is questionable, but it was convenient for Ann, for she could escape from her servile position with her sister. And, it was beneficial for the Major. The sixty-two-year-old gentleman must have been proud of his young and attractive wife. Ann Pryor was apparently a dutiful and respected wife to Major Pryor until she met and fell in love with Charles Frémont. How long they carried on their secret love affair isn't known, but by July 11, 1811, Richmond society was shocked by their scandalous affair when Ann left Major Pryor to live with Frémont. Frémont was dismissed from his position at the academy by Louis Girardin and thereafter until Frémont's death, he and Ann would be wanderers from one city to the next, always living on the edge of poverty. Major Pryor petitioned the Virginia Legislature for a divorce, but it was rejected December 13, 1811.

Into this adventure, and product of these two distinctive people, John C. Frémont was born in Savannah, Georgia, January 21, 1813. Very little is known of his early childhood because of his parent's nomadic life. Moving from Savannah to Nashville, and later to

Norfolk, Frémont's father continued to teach French, paint frescoes, work in dancing schools, take in boarders, and even operated a livery stable. Charles Frémont was able to provide little more than love and affection for his wife and growing family. A daughter died in infancy in Nashville in 1814; a second daughter and second son were born in Norfolk, Virginia, in 1815 and 1817. Tragedy struck the struggling little family when Charles Frémont died in 1818. Ann, left alone to care for the three children, lived for awhile at Dinwiddie Courthouse. But, with an income too small to make life comfortable among her old neighbors and acquaintances, she moved to Charleston, South Carolina, probably in 1820 or 1821. (*Believing that Major Pryor had died by this time, many historians wrote that they were sure Charles and Ann had legally married. However, there is strong evidence that Major Pryor did not die until 1823. Indeed, he was still vigorous enough in 1813 to take the field against the British. The case is very strong that Charles Frémont and Ann W. Pryor could never have been legally married.*)

The move to Charleston was an important event in the young life of the future "Pathfinder." From the stability he was to find there, the friends he was to make, and the lessons he was to learn would emerge an American hero and legend. He was a handsome lad and made friends easily. With a mass of curly dark hair, light blue eyes and olive-colored skin he stood out in any group of young people. His imagination, wit and friendly nature made him popular among all his friends, especially the girls. At the age of fourteen, Frémont, in order to supplement his mother's small income, became a clerk in the law office of John W. Mitchell. Mitchell soon recognized that this lad possessed many talents for one so young. He had an innate refinement and courteous demeanor, an insatiable desire for knowledge and a native ability to understand difficult problems. At the time, young Frémont expressed a desire to become an Episcopal Minister in order to pursue studies in logic, philosophy and classical literature. However, this ambition passed and Mitchell enrolled him and paid his tuition in an excellent preparatory school directed by a scholar from Edinburgh, Dr. Charles Robertson. After two years under Dr. Robertson's tutelage, where he excelled in classical studies and essay writing, Frémont entered Charleston College as a junior. Two years later, shortly before he was to graduate, he was expelled for failure to attend classes. His restlessness, frequent disregard for convention, and impetuosity became evident. And he had fallen in love with a beautiful creole girl named Cecilia. The romance didn't last, however, and Frémont became a teacher at John Wooten's private school. He was seventeen.

Frémont's next encounter with destiny was his good fortune in meeting Joel Roberts Poinsett, the former U.S. Minister to Mexico. As he listened to Poinsett's tales of travel to far and exotic lands, young Frémont was consumed with the desire to see these places. He wanted to break the restraints of Charleston. Poinsett helped him gain an appointment as a mathematics teacher aboard the U.S. Naval Sloop of War, Natchez. (Annapolis Naval Academy was still in the future during these formative years of the U.S. Navy. Midshipmen learned their craft aboard vessels at sea and many subjects relating to their education were taught by civilian teachers under contract, who sailed on the ships with them.) Poinsett, although helping Frémont obtain the appointment, actually did not approve of this decision. He wasn't sure it was the right thing for Frémont to do at this point in his career. Poinsett was probably right. Frémont was to write later of this two-year voyage (1833-35) along the South American Coast, "The time spent was long and had no future bearing."

Upon returning to Charleston at the end of the cruise, Frémont successfully passed a test for a newly created position, Professor of Mathematics in the Navy. He promptly declined the position however, and accepted an offer to accompany Captain W. C. Williams of the U.S. Topographical Corps as an assistant engineer on surveys to be made for a projected railway from Charleston to Cincinnati. With this survey party Frémont was to get his first taste of wilderness exploration. He loved it, and for the next twenty years, 1836 to 1856, he would spend nearly as much time under the stars as under a roof.

Shortly after the railroad survey was completed, Frémont was again employed by Captain Williams in 1837, as an assistant in a military reconnaissance to the Cherokee Indian tribal lands in North Carolina, Tennessee, and Georgia. As he later wrote, "the accident of this employment curiously began a period of years of like work for me among similar scenes. Here I found the path which I was destined to walk. Through many of the years to come the occupation of my prime of life was to be among Indians and waste places. Other events which intervened were incidents in this and grew out of it. There were to be no more years wasted in tentative efforts to find a way for myself. The work was laid out and it began here with remarkable continuity of purpose."

The Cherokee survey over, Frémont secured letters of recommendation from Poinsett, now Secretary of War in President Van Buren's cabinet, and his recent chief, Captain Williams. He applied for a commission in the U.S. Corps of Topographical Engineers in December of 1837. In the meantime he accepted an assignment as civilian assistant, civil engineer, to the distinguished French scientist, Joseph Nicolas Nicollet, who was about to depart on an expedition to the northern territories between the Missouri and Mississippi rivers. Frémont's commission as a Second Lieutenant was approved while he was on this journey.

Joseph Nicollet (1786-1843) was a remarkable mathematician and explorer, and again fate had placed Frémont in the right place at a propitious time in his young career in order to further improve his abilities for the tasks awaiting him. During the two expeditions to the Upper Mississippi and Missouri on which Frémont assisted, Nicollet was a good teacher and Frémont a good pupil. Under Nicollet's tutelage, Frémont quickly learned to deal with frontier traders, Indians and voyageurs. *(Voyageur (vwa-ya-zhur). The voyageurs were usually of French Canadian, Creole, or French-Indian heritage, and most were half-breeds. This hearty, fun-loving, occasionally heroic breed of men were as much a part of the frontier as the Indians during this era. They were accustomed to the deprivations and hardship of travel in the Indian lands. They were the laborers who carried the baggage, manned the oars, and cared for the animals and equipment.)*

He became proficient in land navigation, botany, geology and astronomy. Perhaps most importantly, he learned to accurately sketch the geography of the land and, in truth, become a topographical engineer, capable of exploring and mapping an unknown region.

The first expedition was completed in late 1838. While wintering in St. Louis, the maps and reports were refined in preparation for submission to the government. The second expedition, which was to explore the western area of the Upper Missouri River, began in early April 1839. After many adventures, including getting lost for a short time, and learning more and more the art of wilderness survival, Frémont successfully completed the expedition in the winter of 1840-41. Frémont accompanied Nicollet back to Washington to help with the government reports. Nicollet gave a glowing account of his assistant's ability, energy and conduct. Frémont had earned the compliments.

The year of 1841 was to be significant in furthering Frémont's education and ambition. Working with Nicollet and Lt. Scammon of the Topographical Corps, the finished maps and official congressional report were completed — and, he met Jessie Anne Benton. Frémont wrote, "She was just then in the bloom of her girlish beauty, and perfect health effervesced in bright talk ... Naturally, I was attracted. She made the effect that a rose of rare color or a beautiful picture would have done."

Jessie Benton was only fifteen-years-old when she met her future husband at Mrs. English's private school in Georgetown, but it was love at first sight for both of them. It was the beginning of an eventful love affair that would last for nearly a half-century. A young beauty with dark hair, brown eyes, flawless skin and oval face, Jessie was the daughter of Missouri's senior Senator, Thomas Hart Benton. Accentuating her physical beauty, gaiety and quick wit was her "grasp of mind, comprehending with a quickness of perception and instant realization of subject and scenes in their complete extent ... and a tenderness and sensibility that made feeling take the place of mind," Frémont wrote.

Frémont had met Senator Benton and many high ranking officials through his association with Nicollet. The Senator and the young Lieutenant each developed a liking and respect for the other's intelligence and ambitions for exploring and opening the western frontier for expansion of the United States – Manifest Destiny. This dynamic phrase had not yet been coined. That would come a few years later, in 1845. But in no battle cry has a nation's philosophy been more clearly stated, in it Americans found both recognition and revelation; it was the very core of the American faith and dedication. It was a lofty and noble assumption of purpose and goal by its proponents. An army of emigrants and soldiers would advance beyond the Mississippi and Missouri rivers to the Pacific Coast, spreading the belief that American institutions were superior, and that the free government mode of life and liberty were better for the less fortunate, less happy peoples living in the wilderness and mountains between. They would set an admirable example by such action and by practicing their virtues. Because the United States was a nation bursting at its seams with thousands of restless and adventurous people ready to settle this new land, till the virgin soil, and build new cities, it was a geographically logical route to empire. To the thousands of western native American Indians, to the British Empire and the Government of Mexico, it was simply what it was, an invasion and conquest.

While Jessie was in school and before they met, Frémont spent many memorable evenings in the Benton home. Almost a nightly guest, he was quick to respond to the genuine love Thomas and Elizabeth Benton had for each other and their respect for disciplined work habits and social grace. Lieutenant Frémont had not been in such an atmosphere for many years.

Senator Benton and others had been laying the groundwork for another government expedition further to the west. Joseph Nicollet was to be its leader, but his health was failing rapidly. When it became evident that Nicollet was seriously ill, Frémont was again in the right place at the right time and was the logical choice to conduct the exploration. Years later Senator Benton wrote,

"Frémont did not enter the army through the gates of West Point, and was considered an intrusive officer by the graduates of that institution. Having, before his appointment, assisted for two years the learned astronomer, Mr. Nicollet, in his great survey of the country between the Missouri and Mississippi, his mind was trained to such labor; and instead of hunting comfortable berths about the towns and villages, he solicited employment in the vast regions beyond the Mississippi. That order did not come up to his views. After receiving it he carried it back and got it altered, and the Rocky Mountains inserted, as an object of his exploration, and the South Pass in those mountains named as a particular point to be examined, and its position fixed by him."

There was another reason for sending Frémont away from Washington. John Frémont and Jessie Benton were becoming much too attracted to each other. While working on the plans for the expedition to the west and completing the Nicollet expeditions maps and reports, Frémont and Jessie courted almost daily. They were attentive to little else than each other. Both Senator and Mrs. Benton were opposed to the relationship. Although he was a rising personality, handsome, intelligent, and endowed with social grace, charm and wit, he was still a Second Lieutenant in the Army. It was not a suitable marriage for an attractive and eligible young lady about to enter the very exclusive circles of Washington society. Ironically, Mrs. Benton was the most vehement in her opposition to the young lovers, although she had married Senator Benton under somewhat similar circumstances. Elizabeth Benton's true ambition for her daughter was a marriage to President Martin Van Buren, who had expressed more than a casual interest in young Jessie.

The Bentons sharply curtailed Jessie's meetings with Frémont, but not their love. The problem climaxed on March 4, 1841, at William Henry Harrison's inauguration ceremony. It was obvious to all that the dashing young lieutenant and the lovely Jessie were deeply in love and they made no effort to hide their affection for each other. Later, at home in the library, Benton admonished Jessie that she was too young to marry, and though the family admired Lieutenant Frémont, he was not a proper match for her. He had no money, no family, and prospects for Army promotions would be slow. Shortly thereafter, Senator Benton talked to Frémont and made it quite clear how the family felt and that any thoughts of marriage would have to wait at least a year. This would allow time for Jessie to mature and perhaps find someone more suitable. Reluctantly, both accepted the conditions and except for one memorable evening, seldom saw each other in the ensuing weeks. On April 25, 1842, Lieutenant Frémont received his orders to lead the first U.S. exploring expedition to the Rocky Mountains. Destiny would keep them apart for only a short time.

During the next few months Jessie and her young lieutenant tried desperately to abide by her family's wishes. It was just that neither of them had the temperament for emotional restraint. Frémont was sent back to survey the lower part of the Des Moines River at the insistence of Senator Benton. As soon as he returned, Frémont and Jessie began to secretly meet each other in out-of-the-way places. By October they decided that their personal happiness was more important than anything else. With the assistance of Senator Crittenden's wife, they were secretly married by a Catholic Priest, Father Van Horseigh, probably at the home of Senator Crittenden, on the evening of October 19, 1841. (*There are two versions of where the marriage took place. Some historians have written that the ceremony took place in the parlor of Gadsby's Hotel. The Senator's home is preferable and more logical.*)

They were both Protestants, but neither they nor the Crittendens could find a Minister who would perform the services. Those who were asked, refused, fearing the wrath of the powerful Senator. Immediately after the ceremony they returned to their homes. They continued to meet secretly, but the situation became unbearable. Within a few weeks they determined to face her father, tell the truth, and make the best of whatever happened. Years later, Jessie delighted in telling the story to her grandchildren. Frémont was stammering and embarrassed, but determined. Jessie was as tough and resolute as her father. At first, Senator Benton ordered him out of the house. "Never cross my door again! Jessie shall stay here." Jessie defiantly quoted from the biblical Ruth as she clutched tightly to her husband's arm, "whither thou goest, I will go; and where thou lodgest, I will lodge: thy people shall be my people, and thy God my God."

Benton knew his daughter meant what she said. He capitulated gracefully, and without asking anyone's opinion told his new son-in-law, "go collect your belongings and return at once to the house. I will prepare Mrs. Benton." From that point on, Frémont's destiny was to be linked to one of the most powerful and influential men of that time.

Their marriage was a superb one for that or any other time and they complimented each other as working partners. For the remainder of their lives they would remain faithful and devoted, even to the point of worship. She would inspire him to be exceptional and comfort him when he failed. Neither of them accepted his defeats as anything more than temporary setbacks and when he faltered she was a waiting crutch. When he reached the heights, she publicized his achievements. This relationship was not a common thing then, as it would not be now, but John and Jessie Frémont were not average human beings.

Frémont's first expedition laid the foundation for the focal area of this book; the second expedition. Benton's Senate speech summarizes the first trek, its purposes and accomplishments in an interesting manner:

"Last summer a very interesting expedition had been undertaken to the Rocky Mountains ... ordered by Col. Abert ... and executed by Lieutenant Frémont of the topographical engineers. The objective of the expedition was to examine and report upon the rivers and country between the frontiers of Missouri and the base of the Rocky Mountains; and especially to examine the character, and ascertain the latitude and longitude of the South Pass, the great crossing place to these mountains on the way to Oregon. All the objectives of the expedition have been accomplished, and in a way to be beneficial to science, and instructive to the general reader, as well as useful to the government. Supplied with the best astronomical and barometrical instruments, well qualified to use them, and accompanied by twenty-five voyageurs, enlisted for the purpose at St. Louis, and trained to all the hardships and dangers of the prairies and the mountains, Mr. Frémont left the mouth of the Kansas on the frontiers of Missouri, on the 10th of June; and in the almost incredibly short space of four months returned to the same point, without an accident to a man, and with a vast mass of useful observations, and many hundred specimens in botany and geology. In executing his instructions, Mr. Frémont proceeded up the Kansas River far enough to ascertain its character, and then crossed over to the Great Platte, and pursued that river to it source in the mountains, where the Sweetwater (a head branch of the Platte) issues from the neighborhood of the South Pass. He reached the Pass on the 8th of August, and described it as a wide and low depression of the mountains, where the ascent is as easy as that of the hill on which the capitol stands, and where a plainly beaten wagon road leads to the Oregon through the valley of Lewis' River, a fork of the Columbia. He went through the Pass, and saw the headwaters of the Colorado, of the Gulf of California.and leaving the valleys to indulge in laudable curiosity, and to make useful observations, and attended by four of his men, he climbed the loftiest peak of the Rocky Mountains , until then untrodden by any known human being; and, on the 15th of August, looked down upon the ice and snow some thousand feet below, and traced in the distance the valleys of the rivers which, taking their rise in the same elevated ridge, flow in opposite directions to the Pacific Ocean and to the Mississippi. From that ultimate point he returned to the valley of the Great Platte, following the stream in its whole course, and solving all questions in relation to its navigability, and the character of the country through which it flows. Over the whole course of this extended route, barometrical observations were made by Mr. Frémont, to ascertain latitudes and longitudes; the face of the country was marked as arable or sterile; the facility of travelling, and the practicability of routes noted; the grand features of nature described; ... military positions indicated; ... Eight carts, drawn by two mules each, accompanied the expedition; a fact which attests the facility of travelling in this vast region. Herds of buffaloes furnished subsistence to the men; a short, nutritious grass, sustained the horses and mules. Two boys (one twelve years of age, the other eighteen) besides the enlisted men, accompanied the expedition, and took their share of the hardships; which proves that boys, as well as men, are able to traverse the country to the Rocky Mountains." *(Five men climbed the mountain and reached the summit of the peak with him. Frémont Peak, 13,730 feet in the Wind River Mountain chain is not nearly the highest peak in the Rocky Mountains. There are fifty-four peaks in Colorado over 14,000 feet and Gannet Peak, only a few miles to the northwest of Frémont Peak is 55 feet higher.)*

John Randolph Benton, the Senator's son was the twelve-year-old, and Henry Brant, the son of Colonel J. B. Brant of St. Louis, was the other youth. Senator Benton s remarks concerning the "sharing of the hardships" isn't quite accurate. Young Benton and Brant stayed at Fort Laramie and did not make the trek into the Wind River Mountains. Because of many warnings and reports of marauding hostile Indians west of the fort, Frémont had decided it would be unsafe for them to continue to the South Pass area. The reports were true, but Frémont was able to avoid a confrontation. Kit Carson felt the warnings sufficiently ominous to make out his will.

Senator Benton ended his speech by recommending Frémont's report be published in extra numbers by the Senate in the general interest of the whole country, to science, and the government. The printing was ordered.

Geographers and historians will note a number of inaccuracies and discrepancies in Senator Benton's speech delivered in the Senate, March 2, 1843. Most can be explained as the boasting remarks of a proud father-in-law and new grandfather. Frémont had returned to Washington October 29, 1842, the expedition having begun from St. Louis on May 22. On November 13, Jessie gave birth to their first child, Elizabeth. Although Jessie was disappointed at not having a son as her first-born, Frémont was ecstatic.

The winter of 1842-43 was a glorious one for Frémont and his wife. The proud new parents worked feverishly on his official report of the first expedition. Charles Preuss, his enigmatic cartographer, was to prepare the maps and sketches and Frémont convinced the eminent botanist, Professor John Torrey, to prepare a catalog of the hundreds of plants brought back. The greatest task was Frémont's. The government wanted a full report of what had taken place on the trip. After he had made several unsuccessful beginnings on the narrative, Jessie convinced her husband that she should be his secretary. He would dictate from his notes and she would write, probing and polishing his thoughts as he talked. Jessie had often performed these same duties for her father and she was exceptionally good at it. With Frémont pacing the floor, reliving each day, and Jessie writing furiously, the report, along with the second expedition report, was to become a classic. It was finished for publication on March 1, 1843. Frémont's easy, yet thorough and accurate style, expressing what he saw and felt, was exactly what his superiors and mentors wanted. More importantly, it was what the restless American people preparing to move west wanted and needed. Though a scientific work, it was received enthusiastically by a public craving information, and to this day remains a standard for excellence in its field. On March 10, 1843, Frémont received his orders for a second expedition, this time to connect with the Wilkes' survey in Oregon.

Chapter II

THE SECOND EXPEDITION — ACROSS SOUTH PASS

THREE ACCOUNTS were written about Frémont's second expedition, describing all or part of the journey. Charles Preuss kept a diary, written in his native German. Theodore Talbot also wrote in diary or journal form. And, there was, of course, John Charles Frémont's report. Frémont's narrative will be liberally quoted because it is by far the best reference for the second expedition. Supplemental information is often provided by Preuss, Talbot, and other sources.

The private diaries of Charles Preuss were not found until 1954, when after a thirty-year search Dr. Erwin G. Gudde located them in Berlin, Germany. The Preuss family, realizing the historical importance of the diaries, presented them to the U.S. Library of Congress and subsequently a microfilm of the original was deposited in the Bancroft Library of the University of California. From the microfilm, Dr. and Mrs. Gudde wrote their translated and edited book, "Exploring with Frémont," published by the University of Oklahoma Press in 1958. Ostensibly, Preuss wrote the diaries as a form of communication with his wife, Gertrud. This may have been true in the beginning, but in a very short time Preuss' diary became a personal sanctuary where he could vent his frustrations, dissatisfaction, and unhappiness without irritating his employer and companions.

Charles Preuss, nee George Carl Ludwig Preuss, was Frémont's topographer and cartographer on his first, second and fourth expeditions. Besides his achievements in cartography, he must also be considered one of the outstanding frontier artists of his era. his sketches are amazingly accurate and among the most representative of early western exploration. Born April 30, 1803, in Hoscheid, Germany, this morose and often bitter man was able to hide his true character by transferring his unhappiness to the pages of his diary. Outwardly, he was apparently a calm and pleasant gentleman of intellect. Frémont, Carson, Talbot, and others who wrote or commented about him, did so with great respect and clear affection. In truth, he detested the wilderness and would much rather have been in a comfortable office where he could pursue his endeavors far from the deprivation and hardship of exploration in primitive lands among primitive people. But, he accepted the position with Frémont because he was well paid and was always in need of work when Frémont asked. He was a devoted husband to his wife and a good father to his four daughters. But, as the years went by, his neurotic personality emerged more and more and he suffered periods of deep depression and despondency. He committed suicide by hanging himself on September 1, 1854.

Theodore Talbot's journal of the expedition is a highly readable and youthfully exuberant account, probably intended only for his mother, Adelaide, and unfortunately ends abruptly upon his arrival at Fort Boise. If he wrote anything further about the journey, it has not been found. Talbot's Journal is also in the Library of Congress. It was edited and published by Charles H. Carey in 1931. Also included in the publication are Talbot's journals of his travels to Oregon via Hawaii and his Army responsibilities in Oregon Territory, 1848-1852. He was the son of Isham Talbot, a former Kentucky Senator and a family friend of Colonel J.J. Abert, Commander of the Topographical Corps. Only eighteen-years-old at the time, young Talbot was considering a military career and apparently Abert allowed him to go on the expedition for familiarization purposes. Although he had no official capacity and his expenses and equipment paid for by his family, he often assisted Frémont as a clerk, stood guard duty, and more than measured up as a man capable of shouldering responsibility and work. Apparently enjoying the rigors of frontier life, Talbot later joined the army and did go on to serve honorably in many places before dying of tuberculosis at the age of thirty-seven, April 22, 1862. At the time of his death, he had attained the rank of Major and was an assistant to the Adjutant General of the Union Army. The second expedition led by John C. Frémont may have been conceived in a political conspiracy, born in controversy and nurtured by the majestic mountains and plains of the frontier, but it achieved greatness through the courage and stamina of its leaders and voyageurs. Only occasionally in the course of events does history combine a few bold and talented people, the best available equipment, and a noble purpose. There were a number of individuals employed by Frémont for certain duties on the second expedition who were ill-equipped for the hardships of wilderness exploration. However , it is remarkable that most of the men performed so well and on many occasions heroically. Those who were not suited for this demanding work would eventually drop out along the way. Frémont's narrative begins:

Washington City, March 1, 1845.

Colonel J. J. Abert, Chief of the Corps
of Topographical Engineers:

"Sir: In pursuance of your instructions, to connect the reconnaissance of 1842, which I had the honor to conduct, with the surveys of Commander Wilkes on the coast of the Pacific Ocean, so as to give a connected survey of the interior of our continent, I proceeded to the Great West early in the spring of 1843, and arrived, on the 7th of May, at the little town of Kansas, on the Missouri frontier, near the junction of the Kansas River with the Missouri River, where I was detained near two weeks in completing the necessary preparations for the extended explorations which my instructions contemplated. *[Kansas was also called Kaw Landing or Westport Landing. Today the area is all within Kansas City, Missouri.]*

My party consisted principally of Creole and Canadian French, and Americans amounting in all to 39 men; among whom you will recognize several of those who were with me in my first expedition, and who have been favorably brought to your notice in a former report. Mr. Thomas Fitzpatrick, whom many years of hardship and exposure in the western territories, had rendered familiar with a portion of the country it was designed to explore, had been selected as our guide; and Mr. Charles Preuss, who had been my assistant in the previous journey, was again associated with me in the same capacity on the present expedition. Agreeably to your directions, Mr. Theodore Talbot, of Washington City, had been attached to the party, with a view to advancement in his profession; and at St. Louis, I had been joined by Mr. Frederick Dwight, a gentleman of Springfield, Massachusetts , who availed himself of our overland journey, to visit the Sandwich Islands and China, by way of Fort Vancouver.

The men engaged for the service were: Alexis Ayot, François Badeau, Oliver Beaulieu, Baptiste Bernier, John A. Campbell, John G. Campbell, Manuel Chapman, Ransom Clark, Philibert Courteau, Michel Crelis, William Creuss, Clinton Deforest, Baptiste Derosier, Basil Lajeunesse, François Lajeunesse, Henry Lee, Louis Menard, Louis Montreuil, Samuel Neal, Alexis Pera, François Pera, James Power, Raphael Proue, Oscar Sarpy, Baptiste Tabeau, Charles Taplin, Baptiste Tesson, Auguste

Vasquez, Joseph Verrott, Patrick White, Tiery Wright, Louis Zindel, and Jacob Dodson, a free young colored man of Washington City, who volunteered to accompany the expedition, and performed his duty manfully throughout the voyage. Two Delaware Indians - a fine looking old man and his son - were engaged to accompany the expeditions as hunters, through the kindness of Major Cummins, the excellent Indian Agent .... L. Maxwell, who had accompanied the expedition as one of the hunters in 1842, being on his way to Taos in New Mexico, also joined us at this place. *(Maxwell, Bernier, Menard, Basil Lajeunesse, Proue, and Badeau were with Frémont the previous year on the first expedition. Louis Zindel had been with Frémont during the Nicollet expeditions. Jacob Dodson was an eighteen-year-old servant in the Benton household and was Frémont's body servant during the expedition. Frémont, zealously anti-slavery, would pay a higher wage to Dodson than to the older, and more strenuously engaged voyageurs. The two Delaware Indian hunters were father and son, James Rogers, Sr., and Thomas Jefferson Rogers.)*

The party was armed generally with Hall's carbines, which, with a brass 12-pound howitzer, had been furnished to me from the United States arsenal at St. Louis, agreeably to the orders of Colonel S. W. Kearney, commanding the 3rd military division.

Three men were especially detailed for the management of this piece under the charge of Louis Zindel, a native of Germany, who had been nineteen years a non-commissioned officer of artillery in the Prussian army, and regularly instructed in the duties of his profession. The camp equipment and provisions were transported in twelve carts, drawn each by two mules; and a light covered wagon, mounted on good springs, had been provided for the safer carriage of instruments."

On this expedition, Frémont decided to take a different route to the Rocky Mountains from that followed in 1842. This time instead of going up the Platte River to South Pass, he wanted to take a more southerly route up the valley of the Kansas River. By making this deviation from the former route, he hoped to find a new road to Oregon and California in a better climate.

After receiving Jessie's urgent note, Frémont moved out on May 29, 1843. The journey began in a cold incessant rain, and they camped about four miles beyond the frontier, on the edge of the great prairies. Resuming the journey on the 31st, after a delay of a day to complete the outfitting of the expedition, they camped that evening at Elm Grove, in company with the emigrant wagons of the Chiles-Walker party. Joseph B. Chiles was the leader of the train and that famous frontiersman and mountain man, Joe Walker, was his guide. The emigrant wagons were loaded with goods, furniture, and farming utensils, containing among other things an entire set of machinery for a mill which Chiles intended to build on the Sacramento River. At Elm Grove, Frémont was also joined by William Gilpin, of Missouri, who was going to visit the settlements in Oregon. *(After returning from his journey to Oregon, Gilpin distinguished himself in the Mexican War while serving with Doniphan. In 1847 as a Lieutenant Colonel, he commanded the five companies of "The Battalion.on of Missouri Volunteers," in an expedition against the Cheyenne and Arapaho. Wholly untrained, ineffective, and without the means for negotiation, the Missouri Battalion failed miserably in their mission, but Gilpin escaped any stigma. For the next fifteen years he became a sought after writer and speaker on the West. President Lincoln appointed him the first Governor of Colorado Territory in 1861.)*

For the next few days wagon trains were almost constantly in sight, giving the road the appearance of a well-traveled thoroughfare. Leaving the usual emigrant road where it turned north to the Platte River, Frémont made his way along the south side of the Kansas. The south side of the river was much more broken than the northern side, and their progress was delayed by numerous small streams which where difficult to cross. On the morning of the 4th, they crossed Indian Otter Creek where they met a small party of Kansas and Delaware Indians returning from a hunting and trapping expedition. On the afternoon of the 6th, while busily engaged in crossing a wooded stream, the expedition was thrown into confusion by the sudden arrival of Lucien Maxwell, who rode into camp at full speed running from a war party of Osage Indians. Their heads shaved to the scalp-lock, they had pursued him a distance of about nine miles from a creek where the party had camped the day before. Maxwell had been trying to retrieve Dwight's runaway horse when the war party jumped him. The Osage charged into the camp, drove off a number of the best horses, but after a chase of seven or eight miles, Frémont's men recovered their animals. (*Lucien Bonaparte Maxwell (1818-1875) was at the time a comparatively unknown frontiersman. One year later, through a fortunate marriage, personal courage and ambitiously aggressive business judgment, he would begin building a New Mexico land and livestock empire, the Maxwell Grant. By 1866 he was the sole owner of a princely domain, the largest in the history of the United States, 2,680 square miles or 1,714,764.93 acres, where 500 men were on his payroll herding 1,000 horses, 10,000 cattle and 40,000 sheep, or working in his several gold, silver and copper mines. Although a shrewd businessman and somewhat eccentric, he made hundreds of friends through his generosity and died a respected and well-liked man.*)

As Frémont said, "This accident, which occasioned delay and trouble, and threatened danger and loss, and broke down some good horses at the start, and actually endangered the expedition, was a first fruit of having gentlemen in company — very estimable, to be sure, but who are not trained to the care and vigilance and self-dependence which such an expedition required, and who are not subject to the orders which enforce attention and exertion." (*Frederick Dwight was a Harvard law student who had hoped to travel with the expedition as far as Fort Vancouver, where he might board a vessel bound for Hawaii and China. Frémont's caustic remarks were directed primarily at him, although there were other greenhorns in the party having to learn their way in the wilderness. This was the second horse Dwight had lost, and this one lit out for home with a good saddle, bridle, and pair of pistols. Dwight was a long way from his law books.*)

On the 8th, Frémont arrived at the forks of the Republican and Kansas rivers. Neither stream was fordable, and the necessity of making a raft, together with bad weather, detained them nearly three days before they resumed the journey west along the Republican Fork. For several days Frémont continued to travel along the Republican. Now and then the party caught a glimpse of a small herd of elk, and occasionally a band of antelope, whose curiosity sometimes brought them within rifle range. The country was covered with many varieties of luxuriant and rich grasses. On the evening of the 14th, they camped at a place called Big Timber on a little creek in the valley of the Republican, 235 miles from the mouth of the Kansas. Their progress was extremely slow, the unusually wet spring and constant rain having so saturated the whole country that they averaged only five or six miles a day.

Finding that such a slow rate of travel would make it impossible for him to comply with instructions, Frémont decided to divide the party. Leaving Fitzpatrick in charge of the provisions and heavier baggage of the camp, Frémont went ahead with a party of fifteen men, taking with him the howitzer and the light wagon which carried the instruments. Talbot wrote, Thurs. June 15th. "Did not move camp. Mr. Frémont is going ahead with a small party and we are all making preparations. Our cannoneer was very successful in his practise [sic] with the howitzer, striking a post four feet high at nearly a quarter of mile, with a bomb."

On the morning of the 16th, the parties separated. Under the command of Thomas Fitzpatrick, the baggage and equipment party of twenty-five voyageurs and neophytes took a more northwesterly course from the Kansas River. After reaching the Platte near Grand Island (Nebraska) they turned west along the south bank until coming to the forks, then southwest along the South Fork of the Platte to Fort St. Vrain, arriving July 14, 1843, ten days after Frémont's party.

The fabled "White Hair," or "Broken Hand," Thomas Fitzpatrick was a native of Ireland, born in 1798 or 1799. Coming to the U.S. as a youth, he was soon attracted to the frontier and was employed by General William H. Ashley in 1822. In 1823-24 he was a co-leader with Jedediah Smith of a small party of Ashley trappers that made the first effective discovery of South Pass. The pass had been previously traversed by "The Astorians" under Robert Stuart in 1812, but its significance was unrecognized. With its re-discovery by Smith, Fitzpatrick, James Clyman and eight other trappers in March 1824, this high, broad plateau would for a half-century become the highway to the west used by trappers, traders and emigrants. Fitzpatrick went on to become an integral part of the fur trade era as a trapper and later owner or part-owner of various fur companies from 1823 to 1840. In the early 1840s he was the guide for the first two emigrant wagon trains moving west over the Oregon Trail, and he guided Father De Smet and his missionaries to the lands of the Flathead Indians. He was Frémont's adjutant and guide during the second and third expeditions, and later would guide General S. W. Kearny and his Army of the West. Despite his deserved reputation as an Indian fighter and his many narrow escapes from the scalping knife, he was highly respected by all the tribes of the plains and mountains, and eventually was the first Indian Agent appointed for the nomadic, often hostile, plains tribes.

He received his first sobriquet, "White Hair" in 1832, while enroute to the "Rendezvous" at Pierre's Hole (Teton Valley, Idaho). He was alone when attacked by a war party of Gros Ventre Indians on the western slope of South Pass. Riding for his life, he made for the Wind River Mountains where he hid in the rocks and brush. After losing his horses and guns, he made his way northwest along the Green River Valley toward Pierre's Hole by way of Hoback Canyon and Jackson Hole. Days later he was found by a search party in an emaciated, starving condition, and hardly recognizable. Besides the Gros Ventre, he had also narrowly escaped a pack of hungry wolves. His hair had turned from black to white during this terrifying ordeal, thus "White Hair." The accident to his hand occurred in January 1836, when he again was riding for his life to escape hostile Blackfeet Indians. While trying to find safety and cover on a sand bar in the Yellowstone River, his rifle accidentally discharged and shattered his left wrist. He reloaded and shot two of his attackers. After some weeks of dodging his pursuers he made his way to St. Louis and safety. Thereafter, he was more commonly known as "Broken Hand." At the time of the second expedition, Thomas Fitzpatrick was far more famous west of the Mississippi than any of the others on the expedition . Frémont's report would change this as would the passage of time. Today his name is secure alongside Jedediah Smith, John C. Frémont and Kit Carson. During his era, no man was more widely known for his knowledge of the western frontier or for his personal courage, audacity, energy and stamina. He died at the height of his fame, February 7, 1854, and is buried in Washington, D.C.

Frémont's party moved out in a westerly direction and after a few hours travel over somewhat broken ground, came upon an extensive and high prairie. That evening they camped at a little stream where a single dry tree fueled their supper fires. The road improved as they continued west, the route being generally straight and level. On the afternoon of June 19, they crossed the Pawnee road to the Arkansas. The prairie monotony was dispelled by the appearance of five or six buffalo bulls, forming a vanguard of immense herds through which they traveled for a few days. They struck the South Fork of the Platte on June 30, and arrived at Fort St. Vrain (Colorado) on July 4, during a large Independence Day celebration.

Frémont's animals were worn out, his staple provisions low, and the fort had little of either with which to supply him. Game was plentiful in the area, but he could not proceed into the mountains without healthy animals. Hearing of a large number of mules in Taos (New Mexico), he asked Maxwell, who was leaving the expedition to return to his home there, to purchase twelve mules, pack them with provisions and meet him on the Fontaine-qui-bouit (Boiling Spring River). Before leaving Fort St. Vrain, Frémont discharged his first "tenderfoot," Oscar Sarpy, a man ill-qualified for the hard work of a voyageur, but with enough intelligence to know it. Given a full outfit and provisions, Sarpy returned to the States by way of Fort Laramie. (He may have been the son of one of the Sarpy's of St. Louis, an old and prosperous family of merchants and traders.)

Leaving orders for Fitzpatrick's group to go on to Fort Hall via Fort Laramie and South Pass, Frémont's party then went southwest up the South Fork of the Platte, past Fort Lupton, and first viewed Pike's Peak on July 8. Hungry and searching for game, they turned east down Vermillion Creek and went about fifty miles into Arapaho country before turning back southwest to the hamlet of Pueblo (Colorado), near the confluence of the Boiling Springs and Arkansas rivers. Here he learned of severe Indian troubles in Taos of which Maxwell was unaware when he passed through that country.

Frémont continued: "By this position of affairs, our expectations of obtaining supplies from Taos was set off. I had here the satisfaction to meet our good buffalo hunter of 1842, Christopher Carson, whose services I considered myself fortunate to secure again; and as a reinforcement of mules was absolutely necessary, I dispatched him immediately, with an account of our necessities, to Mr. Charles Bent, whose principal post is on the Arkansas River, about 75 miles below Fontaine-qui-bouit. He was directed to proceed from that post by the nearest route across the country, and meet me with what animals he should be able to obtain at St. Vrain Fort."

Frémont, looking for a guide for the first expedition, had first met Carson in 1842 aboard a steamer going to the upper Missouri River. When Frémont became aware of Carson's credentials as a guide and hunter, he hired him. During the next five years they would share the numerous true adventures that created thousands of myths. These two men liked each other immediately, and working together from 1842 to 1847 suffering the hardships of exploring an often unknown and hostile land, fighting Indians and a war, each developed a great personal respect and deep admiration for the other.

Christopher (Kit) Carson was born December 24, 1809, in Madison County, Kentucky, the son of Lindsey and Rebecca Carson. Most of this large family, ten children at the time with four more to come (five of which were half-brothers and sisters), moved to Boone's Lick, Howard County, Missouri, in 1811. Six years after his father's death in 1818, Kit was apprenticed to learn the saddler's trade, but ran away at age seventeen, joining a wagon train to Santa Fe in August 1826. After three years of working as teamster, cook, and interpreter around Santa Fe, Taos, El Paso, and Chihuahua, he joined Ewing Young's trapping expedition to California in August 1829. For the next two years he learned the trials and rewards of trapping in Arizona streams and the rivers of the San Joaquin and Sacramento valleys. Returning to Taos in April 1831, he met "Broken Hand" Fitzpatrick and joined his Rocky Mountain Fur Company on a trapping expedition up the Sweetwater, across South Pass, up the Green River, into Jackson Hole, then over the Tetons to the Snake River and finally wintering on the Salmon River. In a battle with the Blackfeet, four, perhaps five of his party were killed.

For the next ten years, the short and stocky, grey eyed, blond-headed and bow-legged Kit would work as a free trapper, a company trapper, and a hunter. He would meet and often work with or for most of the famous men of the fur trade era in the Rocky Mountains. As was true with all "Mountain Men," Kit's life was almost a daily adventure just staying alive. Hostile Indians, blizzards, disease, and angry grizzlies killed at least one of every four of these men between 1822 and 1842. Kit's reputation as an "Indian fighter" was hard-earned during his years as a trapper, but well-deserved as he survived many battles.

Carson was one of that rare breed of men who truly deserved to be a "legend in his own time." Frémont's reports made him famous, but his deeds assured him his rightful place in frontier history. Following his years with Frémont and his coming national acclaim, his life would be no less exciting, as he would live one adventure after another, hold many responsibilities and perform needed and dramatic services for his country. Kit died May 23, 1868, loved, respected and honored by his peers and his nation. He was a man of great strength, energy and character; alert, poised, calm in danger, he was among the most courageous of "The Frontiersmen." Perhaps Frémont said it best, "With me, Carson and the truth are the same thing."

After sending Carson to Bent's Fort for supplies, Frémont hired Charles Towne (Town) as a hunter. (*Towne was a well-qualified frontiersman, but suffered terribly a few months later during the winter crossing of the Sierra Nevada. Apaches would kill him and wound Lucien Maxwell in 1848.*) The Frémont party then returned to Fort St. Vrain by a more direct northerly route. During this excursion, he had surveyed to its head one of the two principal branches of the upper Arkansas, seventy-five miles in length, and completed his survey of the South Fork of the Platte. The little cannon was already getting on Preuss' nerves. On July 20, he wrote, "At a bad place the gun carriage of the howitzer broke, and it took time to repair it. If we had only left that ridiculous thing at home."

Frémont's narrative continues: "Reaching St. Vrain's fort on the morning of the 23d, we found Mr. Fitzpatrick and his party in good order and excellent health, and my true and reliable friend, Kit Carson, who had brought with him ten good mules, with the necessary packsaddles. Mr. Fitzpatrick, who had often endured every extremity of want during the course of his mountain life, and knew well the value of provisions in this country, had watched over our stock with jealous vigilance, and there was an abundance of flour, rice, sugar, and coffee, in the camp; and again we fared luxuriously. Meat was, however, very scarce; and two very small pigs, which we obtained at the fort, did not go far among forty men. Mr. Fitzpatrick had been here a week, during which time his men had been occupied in fitting the camp; and the repose had been very beneficial to his animals, which were now in tolerably good condition. Having determined to try the passage by a pass through a spur of the mountains made by the Cache-a-la-Poudre River, which rises in the high bed of mountains around Long's Peak. I thought it advisable to avoid any encumbrance which would occasion detention, and accordingly again separated the party into two divisions — one of which, under the command of Mr. Fitzpatrick, was directed to cross the plains to the mouth of Laramie River and continuing thence its route along the usual emigrant road, meet me at Fort Hall.

"Our Delaware Indians having determined to return to their homes, it became necessary to provide this party with a good hunter; and I accordingly engaged in that capacity Alexander Godey, a young man about twenty-five-years of age, who had been in this country six or seven years, all of which time had been actively employed in hunting for the support of the posts, or in solitary trading expeditions among the Indians. In courage and professional skill he was a formidable rival to Carson, and constantly afterwards was among the best and most efficient of the party, and in difficult situations was of incalculable value. *(Later Frémont would rank Alex Godey with Dick Owens and Kit Carson in bravery and good judgment. He wrote that under Napoleon, these three men would have been Marshals.)* Hiram Powers, [sic. James Power] one of the men belonging to Mr. Fitzpatrick's party, was discharged at this place. *(He was listed and paid as James Power on the official roster and pay voucher.)* A French engage, at Lupton's fort, had been shot in the back on the 4th of July, and died during our absence to the Arkansas. *(Frémont does not mention that the killer was Thomas Fallon and that he was hired by Frémont as a voyageur on July 24, to go with Fitzpatrick's party. Fallon was discharged in Sacramento the following March 14, 1844. Later in 1846 he served in the California Battalion and became Mayor of San Jose, California, in 1851.)* The wife of the murdered man, an Indian woman of the Snake nation, desirous, like Naomi of old, to return to her people, requested and obtained permission to travel with my party to the neighborhood of Bear River, where she expected to meet with some of their villages. She carried with her two children, pretty half-breeds, who added much to the liveliness of the camp. Her baggage was carried on five or six pack horses; and I gave her a small tent, for which I no longer had any use, as I had procured a lodge at the fort. For my own party I selected the following men, a number of whom old associations rendered agreeable to me: Charles Preuss, Christopher Carson, Basil Lajeunesse, François Badeau, J. B. Bernier, Louis Menard, Raphael Proue, Jacob Dodson, Louis Zindel, Henry Lee, J. B. Derosier, François Lajeunesse, and Auguste Vasquez. *(Charles Carey, Talbot's' Journals (1931). Talbot wrote that Alexis Ayot and Philibert Courteau also went with Frémont, as did the Snake Indian widow and her two children. Preuss wrote on September 7, that there were seventeen in the party. This was weeks after the Snake woman and her children had left at Fort Bridger. Preuss also refers twice to "Brandt." No Brandt or anyone similarly named is on the official roster, and neither Frémont nor Talbot mention him. Dr. Gudde mistakenly thought he was one of the Delaware hunters. Apparently it was a nickname or AKA name for one of the voyageurs, and used only by Preuss.)*

After resting his animals for two days, Frémont's party resumed the journey in a northwesterly direction by way of the Cache-a-la-Poudre River and up Poudre Canyon into the Black Mountains (now known as the Laramie Mountains). Crossing the Black and Medicine Bow Mountains, he turned north and camped in the valley of the North Platte nearly equidistant from present-day Sinclair and Saratoga, Wyoming. Knowing they were leaving buffalo country, they killed a number of the animals and were involved in drying the meat when a war party of seventy Arapaho and Cheyenne Indians suddenly appeared. Frémont wrote that the Indians charged the camp intending to attack, and broke off at the last moment when they saw the cannon and his favorable defensive position in a cottonwood grove. After smoking the peace pipe and receiving presents of tobacco and other goods, the war party went on its way. Frémont broke camp on August 6, and continued north, but was delayed the next afternoon when the shaft of the gun carriage broke again. After repairing it they camped the next afternoon on the Sweetwater River, about twenty miles west of Devil's Gate, 315 miles from Fort St. Vrain. While at this camp Preuss wrote, "Aug. 10, shooting buffalo with the howitzer is a cruel but amusing sport." Preuss often lumps several prior incidents into one entry in his diary. It is quite probable that this incident occurred on August 5, during the Indian War Party "visit." It would have been a persuasive method of impressing the Indians with the cannon's killing capability and for procuring much needed meat. His course the next few days would be over familiar ground. He was back on "The Oregon Trail," and would follow it over South Pass.

Frémont writes: "Here passes the road to Oregon; and the broad smooth highway, where the numerous heavy wagons of the emigrants had entirely beaten and crushed the artemisia, was a happy exchange to our poor animals for the sharp rocks and tough shrubs among which they had been toiling so long; and we moved up the valley rapidly and pleasantly.With very little deviation, from our route of the preceding year, we continued up the valley; and on the evening of the 12th encamped on the Sweet Water, at a point where the road turns off to cross to the plains of Green River. *(Note that the "Oregon Trail" was already a well traveled road in 1843.)* Leaving this encampment, (our last on the waters which flow towards the rising sun) we took our way along the upland, towards the dividing ridge which separates the Atlantic from the Pacific waters, and crossed it by a road some miles further south than the one we had followed on our return in 1842. We crossed very near the table mountain, at the southern extremity of the South Pass, which is near twenty miles in width, and already traversed by several different roads.

Selecting as well as I could, in the scarcely distinguishable ascent, what might be considered the dividing ridge in this remarkable depression in the mountain, I took a barometrical observation, which gave 7,490 feet for the elevation above the Gulf of Mexico. You will remember that, in my report of 1842, I estimated that elevation of this pass at about 7,000 feet; a correct observation with a good barometer enables me now to give it with more precision. *(The Summit of South Pass is 7,550 feet. Considering how difficult it is to ascertain the exact highest point on this sloping sage-covered high plain, Frémont's accuracy is noteworthy.)* Its importance, as the great gate through which commerce and travelling may hereafter pass between the valley of the Mississippi and the north Pacific, justifies a precise notice of its locality and distance from leading points, in addition to this statement of its elevation."

Frémont estimated that South Pass was about 1,350 miles from St. Louis by the route up the Platte River and about seventy-five miles less by the Kansas River route. He further estimated that it was another 1,400 miles to the verdant coast of Oregon which would place South Pass near the mid-point of the travelers' journey. Following the route down the Big Sandy River and riding beside the little cannon, Frémont entered the valley of the Green River. For several days they traveled over dry, level and uninteresting plains. On the evening of August 15, they camped in Mexican territory, on the left bank of Green River, sixty-nine miles west of South Pass.

The next day they crossed the Green River by a good ford and continued south along its west bank. Frémont noted that the river was known as the Seeds-ke-dee-agie, or Prairie Hen River a name which it received from the Crow Indians, and that the prairie hen was still abundant. *(Trappers and emigrants were always disappointed to find that these large and beautiful birds were almost inedible. Their meat had a very bitter taste.)* Frémont also commented that further down the Green River from Brown's Hole to the south the river ran through lofty chasms, walled in by precipices of red rock; and even among the wilder tribes who inhabited that portion of the river, it was called the Rio Colorado.

When the Green turned back to the east, Frémont resumed his westerly course passing over high and broken country. About sunset, after a day's travel of twenty-six miles, he reached Black's Fork of the Green River, "a shallow stream, with a somewhat sluggish current, about 120 feet wide wide, timbered principally with willow, and here and there an occasional large tree." He noted that the heavy wagons of the emigrants had so completely pulverized the soil that clouds of fine light dust were raised by the slightest wind, making the road sometimes very disagreeable.

On August 17, Frémont wrote: "Leaving our encampment at six in the morning, we travelled along the bottom, which is about two miles wide bordered by low hills, in which the strata contained handsome and very distinct vegetable fossils. Crossing on the way Black's fork, where it is one foot deep and forty wide, with clear water and a pebbly bed, in nine miles we reached Ham's fork a tributary to the former stream, having now about sixty feet breadth, and a few inches depth of water. *(Frémont has these stream references backward. He came to Ham's Fork first, then came down Black's Fork. Ham's Fork runs into Black's Fork at present-day Granger, Wyoming. Black's Fork runs into the Green about twenty miles south of the town of Green River, Wyoming.)* It is wooded with thickets of red willow, and in the bottom is a tolerably strong growth of grass …. The road here makes a traverse of twelve miles across a bend of the river."

The Shoshone woman left the party on August 18, expecting to find some of her relations at Bridger's Fort, which was only a mile or two distant up Black's Fork. That evening they camped on Salt Creek. Here, one of their mules died and in this portion of their journey they lost six or seven more of their animals.

The grass in the area was very poor and their animals which had been accustomed to grain became weak when they had no other feed than grass. American horses normally were not of any serviceable value until after they had lived a winter in this country and became accustomed to surviving entirely on grass. That evening a cow and calf which had strayed from an emigrant party were found several miles from the road and brought into camp. She was milked and that night the party enjoyed an excellent cup of coffee. That day they traveled twenty-eight miles, and as had been usual since crossing the Green River, the road had been dusty, and the weather smoky and oppressively hot. On August 19, Frémont sent Carson in advance to Fort Hall to make arrangements for a supply of provisions. The next day Frémont noted that his view over a mountainous region was obstructed by "the smoky weather through which the broken ridges were dark and dimly seen." Smoke was a very common obstruction to visibility throughout the frontier mountains and prairies. Emigrant diarists, trappers, soldiers, and explorers often commented on the fires around them or at a distance. Whether caused by nature or man, millions of acres of forest were visibly scarred when Frémont passed through. John W. Powell's 1878 map of Utah Territory shows half of all the timber in the territory had been burned.

Frémont continued: August 21. "An hour's travel this morning brought us into the fertile and picturesque valley of Bear River, the principal tributary to the Great Salt Lake. The stream is here 200 feet wide, fringed with willows and occasional groups of hawthornes. We are now entering a region which for us possessed a strange and extraordinary interest. Where we descended into this beautiful valley it is three to four miles in breadth, perfectly level, and bounded by mountainous ridges one above another, rising suddenly from the plain. We continued our road down the river, and at night encamped with a family of emigrants — two men, women and several children — who appeared to be bringing up the rear of the great caravan. I was struck with the fine appearance of their cattle, some six or eight yoke of oxen which really looked as well as if they had been all the summer at work on some good farm. It was strange to see one small family travelling alone through such a country, so remote from civilization.

The next morning, in about three miles from our encampment, we reached Smith's fork, a stream of clear water, about 70 feet in breadth. It is timbered with cotton-wood, willow, and aspen, and makes a beautiful debouchement through a pass about 600 yards wide between remarkable mountain hills, rising abruptly on either side, and forming gigantic columns to the gate by which it enters Bear River Valley. The edge of the wood, for several miles along the river was dotted with the white covers of emigrant wagons, collected in groups at different camps, where the smokes were rising lazily from the fires around which the women were occupied in preparing the evening meal, and the children playing in the grass; and the herds of cattle grazing about in the bottom, had an air of quiet security, and civilized comfort, that made a rare sight for the traveller in such a remote wilderness. In common with all the emigration, they had been reposing for several days in this delightful valley; in order to recruit their animals on its luxuriant pasturage after their long journey, and prepare them for the hard travel along the comparatively sterile banks of the Upper Columbia." *(Frémont thought this beautiful segment of the Bear River Valley so important to the weary traveler, he had Preuss draw two separate maps depicting the location, trail and terrain.)*

That night Frémont found it necessary to cross a very steep mountain and descend into the valley for water and grass. He groped his way in the darkness down the mountain and reached the river at about 10 o'clock. This incident probably explains the mystery of why Bear Lake is not depicted correctly or named on Frémont's maps. Preuss, never a man to accept or understand personal discomfort wrote, "Last night we traveled in the darkness until ten o'clock. What exploration! What monkey business!" Bear Lake, known as Sweet Lake or Little Lake to the trappers and Indians, is a most beautiful and scenic natural lake. At nearly 6,000 feet elevation, oval shaped and with 8,000 foot and 10,000 foot mountains on three sides, nearly twenty miles long and seven miles wide, it straddles the Utah-Idaho border about twelve miles west of the Wyoming line.

Frémont had crossed the summit of the mountain about seven miles north of the lake, and Preuss did not depict the lake correctly on his map because he apparently could not see it from a favorable vantage point. He drew only what he could see the next morning and Frémont did not comment or name it. And, though difficult to accept, it is possible he didn't know much about the lake or its importance because Fitzpatrick was more than a week behind him and Carson had been sent ahead to Fort Hall. Months later from a freezing, wind-swept 10,000 foot Sierra peak, Preuss would accurately sketch the general configuration of Lake Tahoe fifteen miles distant.

Continuing up Bear River Valley toward Soda Springs, Frémont approached within a mile of an Indian village. Suddenly a single horseman emerged from it at full speed, followed by another, and another, in rapid succession. Then party after party poured into the plain, until, when the foremost rider reached them the whole plain was occupied by a mass of Indian horsemen who came charging down upon them with guns, lances, bows and arrows. Some of the Indians were entirely naked, and others fully dressed for war, with the long red streamers of their war bonnets reaching nearly to the ground, all mingled together in the bravery of savage warfare. They had been thrown into a sudden tumult by the appearance of Frémont's flag, which among these people was regarded as an emblem of hostility. Frémont's party had been mistaken for a Sioux war party. When the Shoshone chief saw the mistake, he quieted the excitement and the whole band escorted Frémont to their camp. In a short time Frémont purchased eight horses, for which he gave in exchange blankets, red and blue cloth, beads, knives, tobacco and the usual other articles of Indian traffic. He also obtained from them a considerable quantity of berries and vegetables which his men needed badly. On August 25, after leaving the Shoshones, Frémont wrote:

"In about six miles travel from encampment, we reached one of the points in our journey to which we had always looked forward with great interest — the famous Beer springs. The place in which they are situated is a basin of mineral waters enclosed by the mountains, which sweep around a circular bend of Bear River, here at its most northern point, and which in the course of a few miles acquires a southern direction towards the GREAT SALT LAKE." *(Soda Springs was a landmark and oasis for Indians, trappers, and emigrants. It was known to the trappers as "Beer Springs," because with a little imagination, the carbonated water had the taste of a light German lager beer. The springs were at the northern big bend of the Bear River, where after flowing over one hundred miles almost due north, the river makes a wide half-circle and flows south, emptying into Great Salt Lake. The springs are now submerged beneath the city reservoir of Soda Springs, Idaho.)* Although somewhat disappointed because the springs did not have the unusual beauty which various descriptions had led him to expect, he found it a place of great interest. Frémont continued, "A traveller in a volcanic region remains in a constant excitement, and at every step is arrested by something remarkable and new. There is a confusion of interesting objects gathered together in a small space. Around the place of encampment the Beer springs were numerous; but, as far as we could ascertain, were entirely confined to that locality in the bottom. In the bed of the river for a space of several hundred yards, they were very abundant; the effervescing gas rising up and agitating the water in countless bubbling columns. In the vicinity round about were numerous springs of an entirely different and equally marked mineral character. In a rather picturesque spot, about 1,300 yards below our encampment, and immediately on the river bank, is the most remarkable spring of the place. In an opening on the rock, a white column of scattered water is thrown up to a height of about three feet. The noise it makes gives the impression of a steamboat in motion and without knowing that it had been already previously so called, we gave to it the name of the Steamboat spring." On August 26, before leaving Soda Springs, Frémont decided not to follow the normal trail to Fort Hall, fifty miles to the north. Instead, he opted to explore the Great Salt Lake. "An examination of the great lake which is the outlet of this river, and the principal feature of geographical interest in the basin, was one of the main objects contemplated in the general plan of our survey, and I accordingly determined at this place to leave the road, and, after having completed a reconnaissance of the lake, regain it subsequently at Fort Hall." Frémont's trip to the Great Salt Lake (August 26 to September 18) may not have been clearly authorized by his orders, but it was easily justified. Preuss indicates it wasn't in the original plan. "Frémont changes his mind every day as usual, we shall now go to Salt Lake because two of our cattle were stolen." Frémont included this mileage in his daily count whereas he had not included the 300 mile round trip to southern Colorado. This information is often overlooked by those computing the miles traveled by the cannon. Frémont's party followed the Bear River south to the vast marshland bordering the Great Salt Lake at the river's mouth. The trek to the lake was a myriad of misfortune, errors of judgment and some questionable decisions. At first they became lost and wandered through a labyrinth of hills and valleys. To further add to their troubles they were drenched by heavy rains and thunder storms which made their route a quagmire. Poorly supplied when they left, a slow uncertain route and lack of game in the area added to their problems. Luckily, they stumbled onto a Snake Indian village where they obtained edible roots and other vegetables. Finally, near exhaustion, they reached the lake and in their leaking India rubber boat rowed to an island near the center of the lake. Preuss sketched his accurate and definitive map of the Great Salt Lake, but incorrectly depicted Utah Lake which he could not see. After Frémont had made his notes on the surrounding area, they returned to shore, but not before nearly being swamped a number of times. Wet and hungry, Frémont's party left Salt Lake on September 10. When they arrived at Fort Hall on September 18, they had traveled over 200 miles from the main trail and suffered terribly. Supply problems, equipment breakdowns, terrible terrain and hostile weather had made this trip a miserable experience. However, from one major point of view it was clearly worth the effort. The map and descriptions of the Great Salt Lake and adjacent areas would inspire Brigham Young and his Mormon followers to select this area as their promised land.

When Frémont left Soda Springs, Fitzpatrick's column was camped on the Green River just above the Big Sandy. Talbot writes, "Dwight left us to go ahead to Fort Hall taking with him his man Clarke and Raimond. He is no great loss, for he had not messed [dined] with us since we left Fort Laramie." Dwight had apparently been a pain in the neck from the first day, and here we have the only indication that there may have been another Black man on the expedition other than Jacob Dodson. "His man Clarke," could indicate a Black servant. Raimond had joined the contingent at Fort Laramie and was traveling only to Fort Hall where his brother worked for the Hudson's Bay Company. Apparently Raimond didn't fare too well with Dwight either; he returned the next day.

Fitzpatrick, Talbot and the baggage party had departed Fort St. Vrain on July 27, in a northerly direction. Skirting the Laramie Mountains, they took a direct route to Fort Laramie, arriving there August 4. Fort Laramie was first built by William Sublette and Robert Campbell as a trading post in 1834. At the time it was called Fort William. Later in 1836, Sublette and Campbell sold their interest to Lucien Fontenelle, Tom Fitzpatrick and the American Fur Company. For a time it was called Fort John on the Laramie until later when it was shortened to Fort Laramie. The fort was at the junction of the Laramie and North Platte rivers about a mile east of the present-day fort. This site should not be confused with the city of Laramie, Wyoming, which is eighty-five miles to the southwest. Leaving on the 6th, they followed the well-traveled trail west. A few days earlier, an Indian chief had asked Talbot if there were any Whites remaining in the east. Since he had seen at least 1,500 emigrants on the trail in just a few months, he couldn't believe anyone was left in the States. Fitzpatrick reached Independence Rock on the 15th and on the 17th Talbot noted Frémont's trail coming in from the south a few miles west of Devil's Gate. Frémont was seven or eight days in front of them. Their loaded carts moving smoothly and most of the party in good spirits, they crossed over South Pass August 21, and camped on the Green River on the 25th. Fitzpatrick then followed the trail southwest to where Bridger and Vasquez were about to build their trading post. Talbot was much impressed by Louis Vasquez and his group of trappers. He was also impressed with Walkara, the Ute chief riding with Vasquez. Had Talbot known Walkara was a renegade killer, slave trader and accomplished horse thief, he might have been more wary. With Jim Beckwourth, Peg-Leg Smith and about 50 of his warriors, Walkara made at least two raids into Southern California where they stole over 5,000 horses from the Californians (1835-1839). Turning back northwest, crossing to the Bear River and following Frémont's route, they arrived at Soda Springs, September 9. Talbot got a good view of Bear Lake on the 7th and noted, "on descending, we found ourselves in a long valley with hills on either side. At the far southern extremity of this valley, we could see the waters of the "Little Lake" on Bear River! It is nearly encompassed by mountains and is celebrated for its beautiful scenery and fine mountain trout." Fitzpatrick rested his contingent and enjoyed the springs until the 11th, when he resumed the trek. Moving north to the Portneuf River, they followed the trail to Fort Hall, camping there September 13. Frémont's party arrived at the camp on the 18th.

Fort Hall was built by Nathaniel Wyeth in 1834. Wyeth was probably the unluckiest of all the "booshways" to enter the fur trade, as he was continually frustrated in his plans for achievement and empire. He sold his fort to the Hudson's Bay Company in 1836. It was first built near the confluence of the Portneuf and Snake rivers, but when Frémont passed through it had been moved about ten miles north up the Snake. Before leaving Fort Hall, Frémont convinced his ten weakest men to accept their discharge. The early approach of winter, often poor and uncertain supplies, and severe and treacherous country ahead were good reasons for those who had had enough. Unfortunately, one of Frémont's best and one of his favorites also had to take his discharge — Basil Lajeunesse. His wife's illness and other family problems forced him to return home. Faithful and capable, Basil would later accompany Frémont on his third expedition and would be brutally murdered by Klamath

Indians on May 9, 1846. The men were paid through November 20, their estimated travel time to St. Louis. It would be grossly unfair to refer to these men as quitters or weaklings. The rigors of their journey had been formidable and the trials ahead would test human endurance unmercifully. Perhaps it is best to say that they were less strong than the others at that time. (*This contingent did not return to St. Louis until November 30. They were: August Vasquez, Basil and François Lajeunesse, John A. Campbell, Clinton De Forrest, Michael Creely, Alexis Pera (Parraw), Baptiste Tesson, Patrick White, Henry Lee and William Creuss.*)

Christopher (Kit) Carson as a Union Colonel. Photo taken in St. Louis, Missouri 1864.

Museum of New Mexico Santa Fe

FROM FORT HALL TO SATAN'S PLAYGROUND – THE GREAT BASIN

REPROVISIONED, equipment repaired and men rested, the expedition moved west from Fort Hall on September 22, 1843. Frémont had no trouble obtaining oxen and provisions (sugar, coffee, flour, and butter). This was not true for the Chiles-Walker wagon train, however. The Hudson's Bay Company was becoming increasingly concerned with the numbers of American settlers entering British Territory and they began to discourage them by refusing supplies. Frémont had camped with these emigrants shortly after leaving Westport.

The expedition left the low, rich bottomland around the fort, and followed the Snake River west into a barren basaltic wasteland. (*Charles Preuss wrote, "September 24. - A wild country! How old man Vulcan has played havoc here - a little mythology is quite proper. I sketched a rather pretty waterfall today ... October 2. The Snake River is interesting, I must confess, no matter how awful the country around it may be. The most beautiful little waterfalls, twenty or forty feet high. Then steep, volcanic, rocky shores along which one can travel for days without being able to find a place to get down to the stream. This and the lack of grass makes traveling very difficult."*) Often slowed by heavy rains, snow, swollen creeks and rough and rocky terrain, they camped at American Falls on the 24th. On the 27th, Frémont decided again to separate the party: "Since leaving the American Falls, the road had frequently been very bad; the many short, steep ascents, exhausting the strength of our worn-out animals, requiring always at such places the assistance of the men to get up each cart, one by one; and our progress with twelve or fourteen wheeled carriages, though light and made for the purpose, in such a rocky country, was extremely slow; and I again determined to gain time by a division of the camp. Accordingly, today the parties again separated, constituted very much as before — Mr. Fitzpatrick remaining in charge of the heavier baggage."

Frémont continued following the Snake River and reached Fort Boise on October 9. He was received hospitably by François Payette, the Hudson's Bay Company post master. Crossing the Snake, Frémont now entered present-day Oregon and bearing north-northwest, headed for Fort Walla Walla across the Blue Mountains. The journey was made difficult by thick forests and a poorly defined trail. They reached Dr. Whitman's mission on the 24th and got their first view of the Columbia River the next day. Frémont was impressed: "The appearance of the post and country was without interest, except that we here saw, for the first time, the great river on which the course of events for the last half century has been directing attention and conferring historical fame. The river is, indeed, a noble object, and has here attained its full magnitude. About nine miles above, and in sight from the heights about the post, is the junction of the two great forks which constitute the main stream - that on which we had been travelling from Fort Hall, and known by the names of Lewis's fork, Shoshonee, and Snake River; and the North fork, which has retained the name of Columbia, as being the main stream." (*Old Fort Boise was on the Snake River about one mile south of the mouth of the Boise River, which is approximately eighty miles northwest of present-day Boise, Idaho.*)

With eight fresh horses and increased provisions of dried salmon, potatoes and beef, Frémont departed for The Dalles of the Columbia on October 28. The road was a bad one of very loose, deep sand until November 2, when they took a more inland route south of the river. Reaching The Dalles on the 4th, Frémont writes: "In a few miles we descended to the river, which we reached at one of its remarkably interesting features, known as the Dalles of the Columbia. The whole volume of the river at this place passed between the walls of a chasm, which has the appearance of having been rent through the basaltic strata which form the valley rock of the region. At the narrowest place we found the breadth, by measurement, 58 yards, and the average height of the walls above the water 25 feet; forming a trough between the rocks; whence the name, probably applied by a Canadian voyageur. The mass of water, in the present low state of the river, passed swiftly between, deep and black, and curled into many small whirlpools and counter currents, but unbroken by foam, and so still that scarcely the sound of a ripple was heard. The rock, for a considerable distance from the river, was worn over a large portion of its surface into circular holes and well-like cavities, by the abrasion of the river, which, at the season of high waters, is spread out over the adjoining bottoms. In a recent passage through this chasm, an unfortunate event had occurred to Mr. Applegate's party, in the loss of one of their boats, which had been carried under water in the midst of the Dalles, and two of Mr. Applegate's children and one man drowned. (*Only one of Applegate's children died in the accident mentioned by Frémont. The other boy was his nephew.*) At the time, it would appear from his narrative and maps that Frémont considered The Dalles to be the western terminus of his expedition. He writes that he thought the Wilkes' survey had come that far up the Columbia. It had not, although the Wilkes' map of the area is surprisingly accurate. Hudson's Bay Company records indicate Wilkes obtained most or all of his cartographic information from officers of the Hudson's Bay Company at Fort Vancouver, especially Dr. McLoughlin, Michel Laframboise and James Douglas.

The Wilkes Expedition was a noteworthy U.S. Naval accomplishment. With a squadron of ships (the number varied during the voyage, but was usually five), Lieutenant Wilkes' five-year cruise was of immense value to the Navy and U.S. Government in attaining its objectives, especially the mapping of the South Seas. Only Chapters IV, V and VI of Volume V of his report deal with the exploration of the Pacific Coast. It is also unfortunate that Lt. Wilkes' literary talents were limited. His narrative is poorly arranged and often difficult to understand, and this obscures the expeditions many fine accomplishments. (*In his 1841 report, Michel Laframboise noted that he had helped Lt. Wilkes on several occasions with food, equipment and descriptions of the area of his Hudson's Bay Company fur trapping expeditions to the Sacramento and San Joaquin valleys.*) In the summer and fall of 1841, Lt. Wilkes separated his expedition into four groups. One force explored Puget Sound and later joined the second group which went south from Fort Vancouver overland through the Willamette Valley, over the Cascades, and down the Sacramento River to San Francisco. Another contingent went up the Sacramento from San Francisco to the vicinity of Redding, California. During this time, Lieutenant Wilkes and the remaining contingent sailed up the Columbia River to Fort Vancouver. All the expedition units reunited at Sausalito on San Francisco Bay by October 28, 1841. Sailing by way of Hawaii, the Philippines, Malaysia, and South Africa, they returned to New York on June 10, 1842. (*The voyage began with six ships, but in the ensuing years, two ships were wrecked and one sent home. The Oregon was purchased while at Astoria, Oregon, as a replacement for the wrecked Peacock.*)

Historians have discussed and debated on how much Frémont knew about the Wilkes' Expedition. Undoubtedly, Senator Benton was able to ascertain some of its scope, but to what extent is pure conjecture. Lieutenant Wilkes' report wasn't finished until late in 1844, and wasn't published until after Frémont's report in 1845. The U.S. Army and Navy were as competitive for fame and funds then as they are now. When Wilkes returned, Frémont was on his first expedition. While Wilkes was writing his lengthy report, Frémont was engaged in his second expedition and writing his report. It is doubtful if either of these men knew much about the other or their respective ventures. They were much too involved in their individual duties and responsibilities.

Frémont decided to continue on to Fort Vancouver to obtain supplies for his journey back to the States. Taking only Preuss, Bernier, Dodson, and Indian guides, he traveled by canoe down the Columbia. Cordially received and reprovisioned, Frémont reluctantly departed November 10, to return to The Dalles. (He wanted to continue down river to the Pacific, but could not justify such sight seeing.) It is also apparent that he was informed at Fort Vancouver that Wilkes had not gone further up river, as Frémont then indicated Fort Vancouver as his western terminus. The voyage back up the Columbia was a much more arduous task than going down, but Frémont and the supplies arrived safely back at The Dalles on the afternoon of November 18. Fitzpatrick and the remainder of the party arrived on the 21st. While encamped at The Dalles, John G. Campbell took his discharge as a voyageur and Frémont hired a nineteen-year-old Chinook Indian, William Perkins, to take his place. Leaving the instrument wagons at the Methodist Mission, Frémont started south along the Deschutes River about noon on November 25. The howitzer was the only wheeled vehicle now remaining and they were heading for a vast unexplored territory — The Great Basin. Frémont had first named this arid land between the Rocky Mountains and Sierra Nevada, comprising mostly the State of Nevada, on October 13. He knew that others had traversed some segments of the area, but there had never been any definitive maps or descriptions of the region published.

Jedediah Smith, Silas Gobel, and Robert Evans were the first white men to cross the central part of the Great Basin. Starting from Smith's camp near Murphys, California, these courageous men went east over the Sierra Nevada near Ebbetts Pass, across central Nevada and up to Bear Lake in northeast Utah. From late May until July 4, 1827, they overcame every obstacle and cruelty primitive man and nature could put in their path. It was an Homeric trek.

Joe Walker led B.L.E. Bonneville's party of trappers west from Salt Lake in 1833, traveling down the Humboldt River to present-day Lovelock, Nevada, where they turned almost due south into the Owens Valley of California, and crossed into the San Joaquin Valley by way of Walker Pass or Tehatchapi Pass. They returned by much the same route in 1834. Peter Skene Ogden and his Hudson's Bay trappers had trapped the Humboldt and its tributaries in 1828-29. His party also traversed western Nevada, north to south, in 1829-30, enroute to trap the Colorado River along the border of California and Arizona. In September of 1843, Joe Walker and the largest segment of the Chiles-Walker party left Fort Hall within a few days of Frémont's departure for Fort Vancouver. Walker's group somehow missed the Goose Creek cutoff across Park Valley, Utah, and instead went by way of Calder Creek and the Raft River Valley to the Humboldt River near its headwaters in northeast Nevada. They then followed Walker's previous 1833-34 trail to California, using Walker Pass over the southern tip of the Sierra Nevada. Certainly, other trapping parties had been on the Humboldt. Kit Carson and Alex Godey were there in 1836. Jedediah Smith undoubtedly drew several crude maps of his travels while trapping and exploring the western frontier from 1823 to 1831. And, although the originals are now lost, a few map makers must have had access to them. The 1834 Brue map of the western United States, the 1836 Gallatin map of North American Indian Tribes, the 1839 Burr map of the United States, and the 1841 Wilkes map of Oregon Territory all contain routes and references to Smith. Smith's untimely death when killed by Comanches on May 27, 1831, created a cartographic void that would not be corrected for nearly fifteen years. Michel Laframboise and John Work led Hudson's

Bay Company fur trapping expeditions from Fort Vancouver south through the Sacramento and San Joaquin valleys in 1832 and 1833. Their southernmost camp was usually French Camp near Stockton, California. Starting in 1834, Laframboise led the expeditions himself for the next ten consecutive years. In his annual reports for each of these endeavors he always identified the area as the Valley of the Buenaventura, and consistently identified the San Joaquin River and at least fifty miles of the Sacramento River as the Buenaventura River. It is not known which maps Frémont carried with him, but any or all of the best maps available would have been of little or no use to him for his route of return. For the most part he had to depend on Fitzpatrick and Carson. Undoubtedly, Dr. John McLoughlin at Fort Vancouver had provided considerable information to Frémont on the Laframboise and Odgen expeditions, and surely some knowledge of Jedediah Smith. McLoughlin, a dignified, highly respected physician and administrator, had been in charge of the Columbia district of Hudson's Bay Company since 1824 and had access to more knowledge of the Great Basin than anyone, except for those who had actually been there.

Frémont recorded his return destination plans and route on the 18th: "The camp was now occupied in making the necessary preparations for our homeward journey, which, though homeward, contemplated a new route, and a great circuit to the south and southeast, and the exploration of the Great Basin between the Rocky Mountains and the Sierra Nevada. Three principal objects were indicated, by report or by maps, as being on this route; the character or existence of which I wished to ascertain, and which I assumed as landmarks, or leading points, on the projected line or return. The first of these points was the Tlamath lake, on the tableland between the head of Fall River [Deschutes], which comes to the Columbia, and the Sacramento, which goes to the bay of San Francisco; and from which lake a river of the same name makes its way westwardly direct to the ocean. This lake and river are often called Klamet, but I have chosen to write its name according to the Indian pronunciation. From this lake our course was intended to be about southeast, to a reported lake called Mary's, at some days' journey in the Great Basin; and thence, still on southeast, to the reputed Buenaventura river, which has had a place in so many maps, and countenanced the belief of the existence of a great river flowing from the Rocky mountains to the bay of San Francisco."

Whether Frémont actually believed the mythical Buenaventura River existed is speculative. The romantic in him would certainly want it to exist, but the scientist side of him would have known that all evidence was to the contrary. Sen. Benton's subsequent avowal that Dr. McLaughlin had shown Frémont the river's probable location is a political justification at best. If Senator Benton's statements were true, McLoughlin was certainly referring to the San Joaquin and Sacramento rivers. Dr. McLoughlin knew from Smith's, Laframboise's and Ogden's explorations that a river from the Great Basin to the Pacific Ocean did not exist, and he was much too honorable a man to say otherwise. (For anyone wanting to let their imagination run wild, there was a great river running north to south which the western slope of the Sierra Nevada now covers. This river was as large as the Columbia, and was in existence for about 59 million years before the last Sierra upheaval of about one million B.C. It was from the gravel bed of this river that so many millions of dollars in gold were mined by the giant hydraulic monitors during the gold mining era in California.)

From the Buenaventura, Frémont intended to go due east to the Rocky Mountains and to the head of the Arkansas River, then down the Arkansas to Bent's Fort, and home. This projected line of return, most of it new to geographical, botanical and geological science, would have added considerable knowledge about the rivers, deserts and Indian tribes of the region. Frémont wrote: "It was a serious enterprise, at the commencement of winter, to undertake the traverse of such a region, and with a party consisting only of twenty-five persons, and they of many nations American, French, German, Canadian, Indian, and colored; and most of them young. Several being under twenty-one years of age. All knew that a strange country was to be explored, and dangers and hardships to be encountered; but no one blanched at the prospect. On the contrary, courage and confidence animated the whole party. Cheerfulness, readiness, subordination, prompt obedience, characterized all; nor did any extremity of peril and privation, to which we were afterwards exposed, ever belie, or derogate from, the fine spirit of this brave and generous commencement." *(Throughout the chronicles of the second expedition and his writings on the others, Frémont appears compelled and seldom fails to eruditely comment that all of his major decisions are received with joyous adulating agreement by his men. For self-aggrandizement his comments may have been effective; factual reporting they were not. Historians recognize early on that military and political leaders often justify their actions and decisions in published articles, autobiographies or memoirs. All lost battles are caused by superior overwhelming forces, incompetent subordinates, or the wrath of nature and its elements. All great victories are the result of the leader's brilliant strategy.)*

Frémont went on to explain why he wasn't able to complete this plan. After having made considerable progress, he was forced by desert hardships, mountain ranges and lame animals to change his mind and cross the Sierra Nevada into California. For the support of the party making the return journey, he was provided at Fort Vancouver with a three month's supply of provisions. Additionally, he had purchased at the mission a number of cattle, which were to be driven on the hoof. He had 104 mules and horses, many of which were bought from the Indians at the mission and which could better live and travel on available natural forage. For the next three weeks Frémont and his men moved south through what is now central Oregon. On December 10, Preuss wrote, "Here I am in the mountains, sitting on an old fir trunk, with thin snow around me and a mule beside me, waiting for the caravan. I had to give up my place in the wagon. Frémont said that progress was too slow on the bad roads and gave the wagon away. Yet the cannon causes just as much delay, and unless he presents it to someone as he did the wagon, we shall move ahead slowly."

By December 14, they had reached an area about twenty-five miles north of Klamath Lake, where they turned east, camping at Lake Abert on December 20. *(The lake was named for Col. J.J. Abert, Chief of the U.S. Topographical Corps. It is always good for a young Second Lieutenant to name a lake after his Commanding Officer and Col. Abert was probably pleased. However, had he known that the water was brackish and nearly undrinkable, he might have taken offense. Preuss' diary entry for Dec. 21, was succinct, short, and anything but subtle: "Drank stinking salt water at Abert Lake.")* By Christmas they were at the Warner Lakes.

December 25. "We were roused, on Christmas morning, by a discharge from the small arms and howitzer, with which our people saluted the day; and the name of which we bestowed on the lake. It was the first time, perhaps, in this remote and desolate region, in which it had been so commemorated. Always, on days of religious or national commemoration, our voyageurs expect some unusual allowance; and, having nothing else, I gave them each a little brandy, (which was carefully guarded, as one of the most useful articles a traveller can carry,) with some coffee and sugar, which here, where every eatable was a luxury, was sufficient to make them a feast. The day was sunny and warm, and, resuming our journey, we crossed some slight dividing grounds into a similar basin, walled in on the right by a lofty mountain ridge."

Returning to their general southerly route, Frémont crossed the present-day Nevada state line about ten miles east of the California border. The terrain had been difficult and their labors hard, but they were easy compared to what was in front of them for the next two months. One day they would be in fine powdery sand, the next climbing over snow and ice covered rocks, and for nearly a week the fog was so thick they could hardly see. On January 9, 1844 Frémont wrote: "Our situation now required caution. Including those which gave out from the injured condition of their feet, and those stolen by the Indians, we had lost, since leaving the Dalles of the Columbia, fifteen animals; and of these, nine had been left in the last few days. I therefore determined, until we should reach a country of water and vegetation, to feel our way ahead, by having the line of route explored some fifteen or twenty miles in advance, and only to leave a present encampment when the succeeding one was known." *(This was a good plan which he probably should have started earlier. He had lost considerable time and sapped the strength of his men and animals by unnecessary wandering.)*

On January 10, with a warm sun melting the snow, Frémont discovered and named Pyramid Lake: "Beyond, a defile between the mountains descended rapidly about two thousand feet; and, filling up all the lower space, was a sheet of green water, some twenty miles broad. It broke upon our eyes like the ocean. The neighboring peaks rose high above us, and we ascended one of them to obtain a better view. The waves were curling in the breeze, and their dark-green color showed it to be a body of deep water. For a long time we sat enjoying the view, for we had become fatigued with mountains, and the free expanse of moving waves was very grateful. It was set like a gem in the mountains, which, from our position, seemed to enclose it almost entirely. At the western end it communicated with the line of basins we had left a few days since; and on the opposite side it swept a ridge of snowy mountains, the foot of the great Sierra. Part of the morning was occupied in bringing up the gun; and, making only nine miles, we encamped on the shore, opposite a very remarkable rock in the lake, which had attracted our attention for many miles. It rose, according to our estimate, 600 feet above the water; and, from the point we viewed it, presented a pretty exact outline of the great pyramid of Cheops. Like other rocks along the shore, it seemed to be encrusted with calcareous cement. This striking feature suggested a name for the lake; and I called it Pyramid lake."

Leaving Pyramid Lake on January 16, Frémont continued south along the Truckee River, camping that night near present-day Wadsworth, Nevada. At the time he named it the Salmon Trout River, after he had traded for a huge stock of these succulent fish from the Paiute Indians living there. Now the fish are known as cutthroat trout. On the 18th, while camped on the Carson River near where Fort Churchill would later be built, Frémont decided to abandon his intention of a winter return to the States: "Examining into the condition of the animals when I returned into the camp, I found their feet so much cut up by the rocks, and so many of them lame, that it was evidently impossible that they could cross the country to the Rocky mountains. Every piece of iron that could be used for the purpose had been converted into nails, and we could make no further use of the shoes we had remaining. I therefore determined to abandon my eastern course, and to cross the Sierra Nevada into the valley of the Sacramento, wherever a practicable pass could be found. My decision was heard with joy by the people, and diffused new life throughout the camp."

Although Frémont inserts this decision in the narrative on January 18, it is quite probable that he didn't make it until five or six days later when his animals were in much worse condition. And, there is always the lingering suspicion that California was and had been his real objective. This is conjectural, but he had a number of options more desirable than a mid-winter crossing of the Sierra Nevada. The most obvious being a return to the meadows on the Truckee River south of Pyramid Lake. There, he could have spent an enjoyable winter with plenty of food for his men and animals. The Paiute Indians would have almost certainly showed him the way over Donner, Henness, or Yuba passes, any one of which he could have crossed in late March or early April. And, probably with very little snow, if any, to overcome.

The winter of 1843-44 in the Sierra had below average snowfall. The snow melt and runoff is far different at 5000 to 7000 feet than it is at 8000 feet and above.

Ostensibly still searching for the Buenaventura River, Frémont continued south until the 24th, when he camped about twenty miles southwest of Hawthorne, Nevada. The next day he turned west, passing through the Bodie Hills which a few years later would yield millions in gold. Coming down Aurora Canyon, he camped on the East Walker River at or very near present day Bridgeport, California. Resting his men and animals until the 27th, he then moved northwest up Huntoon Valley and camped on Swauger Creek approximately one mile north of U.S. Highway 395. On the 28th, they passed through Devil's Gate, observed Fales Hot Springs, and turned north across Burcham Flat, camping that night near the top of an 8,420-foot mountain, 2,000 feet above and east of the West Walker River. The next day, January 29, 1844, Frémont was forced to abandon his howitzer. The little cannon could go no farther because of deep snow, savage terrain, tired men and starving animals. Frémont would continue on north, until from the East Carson River on February 2, he would begin an assault on the Sierra Nevada that may have been poor in concept, but was heroic in its accomplishment. It was an emaciated group of men leading skeleton animals who arrived at Sutter's Fort (Sacramento, California) on March 8, 1844. *[The men who made this remarkable crossing of the Sierra were: 1. John C. Frémont, 2. Thomas Fitzpatrick, 3. Christopher Carson, 4. Charles Preuss, 5. Theodore Talbot, 6. Alexis Ayot, 7. François Badeau, 8. Oliver Beaulieu, 9. Baptiste Bernier, 10. Philibert Courteau, 11. Louis Menard, 12. Baptiste Derosier, 13. Louis Montreuil, 14. Samuel Neal, 15. François Pera (Parraw), 16. Raphael Proue, 17. Baptiste Tabeau, 18. Charles Taplin, 19. Joseph Verrot, 20. Tiery Wright, 21. Louis Zindel, 22. Thomas Fallon, 23. Jacob Dodson, 24. Alex Godey, 25. William Perkins, 26. Charles Town (Towne).]* Frémont would go on to successfully complete his second expedition, and achieve, and lose, fame and fortune.

Oliver Beaulieu, Philibert Courteau, Baptiste Derosier, Samuel Neal, Joseph Verrot and Thomas Fallon stayed at Sutter's Fort and did not continue with the expedition. Beaulieu and Courteau were discharged for stealing sugar. Neal became Sutter's blacksmith and later had a large ranch on Butte Creek north of the Sutter Buttes. Fallon later became the Mayor of San Jose. Derosier became lost and nearly went insane wandering in the Sierra a few days before the party made it to Sutter's Fort. He was later found, recovered his health and returned to Missouri. The author has been unable to trace Joseph Verrot from Sutter's Fort. On the return trip to St. Louis tragedy struck three of the voyagers. Baptiste Tabeau was killed and mutilated by desert Indians, May 9, 1844. Two weeks later François Badeau accidentally shot and killed himself. Alexis Ayot accidentally shot and crippled himself for life, July 20, 1844.

We will stay above the West Walker River, on a mountain, and walk up and down some rough canyons. That is where he left the cannon, and that is where it still is.

CELILO FALLS - THE DALLES OF THE COLUMBIA RIVER.
Now deep beneath the waters of the lake formed byThe Dalles Dam.
Photo: Martin Luman

FORT VANCOUVER 1845

Chapter IV

THE CANNON IS ABANDONED

FRÉMONT accurately described the important landmarks along his route of January 26-29, 1844. The expedition had camped on the East Walker River near Bridgeport, California, the nights of January 25 and 26. While the party rested on the 26th, Frémont and Carson explored ahead to the Swauger Creek campsite of January 27. Frémont wrote: "Entering the range, we continued in a northwesterly direction up the valley, which here bent to the right [Huntoon Valley]. From the fresh trails which occurred frequently during the morning, deer appeared to be remarkably numerous on the mountain. We had now entirely left the desert country, and were on the verge of a region which, extending westward to the shores of the Pacific, abounds in large game, and is covered with a singular luxuriance of vegetable life. The little stream grew rapidly smaller, and in about twelve miles we had reached its head, the last water coming immediately out of the mountain on the right, and this spot was selected for our next encampment [Swauger Creek]. *(Frémont probably does not intend to indicate this campsite was at the spring on the side of this steep mountain. He did want to camp in the narrow little valley where the party was protected from cold winds and where there was plenty of grass for the animals. The actual campsite was probably no more than one or two miles up the canyon from U.S. 395.)* To the left, the open valley [Pimentel Meadow] continued in a southwesterly direction, with a scarcely perceptible ascent, forming a beautiful pass; the exploration of which we deferred until the next day, and returned to the camp."

On January 27, Frémont and Thomas Fitzpatrick rode ahead of the main body. This day, Frémont's narrative would forever confuse the exact route of travel. Preuss' map provides the path of the actual route taken and is one of the keys to unlocking the mystery of where the cannon was abandoned. Frémont wrote:

January 27. "Leaving the camp to follow slowly, with directions to Carson to encamp at the place agreed on, Mr. Fitzpatrick and myself continued the reconnaissance. Arriving at the head of the stream, we began to enter the pass — passing occasionally through open groves of large pine trees, on the warm side of the defile, where the snow had melted away, occasionally exposing a large Indian trail. Continuing along a narrow meadow, we reached in a few miles the gate of the pass, where there was a narrow strip of prairie, about fifty yards wide, between walls of granite rock [Devil's Gate]. On either side rose the mountains forming on the left a rugged mass, or nucleus, wholly covered with deep snow, presenting a glittering and icy surface. This was the icy and cold side of the pass, and the rays of the sun hardly touched the snow. On the left, the mountains rose into peaks; but they were lower and secondary, and the country had a somewhat more open and lighter character. On the right were several hot springs, which appeared remarkable in such a place [Fales Hot Springs]. In going through, we felt impressed by the majesty of the mountain, along the huge wall of which we were riding. Here there was no snow; but immediately beyond was a deep bank, through which we dragged our horses with considerable effort. We then immediately struck upon a stream, which gathered itself rapidly, and descended quick; and the valley did not preserve the open character of the other side, appearing below to form a canon. We therefore climbed one of the peaks on the right, leaving our horses below; but we were so much shut up, that we did not obtain an extensive view, and what we saw was not very satisfactory and awakened considerable doubt. *(They climbed the steep escarpment up to Burcham Flat. If they had more time, they could have gone a little further and had a much better view of the West Walker River Canyon.*) The valley of the stream pursued a northwesterly direction, appearing below to turn sharply to the right, beyond which further view was cut off. It was, nevertheless, resolved to continue our road the next day down this valley, which we trusted still would prove that of the middle stream between the two great rivers." (*This single sentence has been the cause of considerable controversy among historians tracing Frémont's route. Those who believe he did continue down the canyon and go over into Mill Valley use it as authentication. Those who believe this was not the route dismiss the sentence as a thought Frémont put in his notes on the 27th and somehow forgot to remove from the finished narrative. He certainly did not take this route. They did not continue down the valley, as Preuss' map clearly shows. To have continued down the Little Walker, cross the West Walker, go up and over the high ridge to Lost Cannon Canyon or into Mill Valley would have been nearly impossible.*)

January 28. "Today we went through the pass with all the camp, and after a hard day's journey of twelve miles, encamped on a high point where the snow had been blown off, and the exposed grass afforded a scanty pasture for the animals. Snow and broken country together made our travelling difficult; we were often compelled to make large circuits, and ascend the highest and most exposed ridges, in order to avoid snow, which in other places was banked up to a great depth."

After passing through Devil's Gate, Frémont's party took the only logical route to the north — across Burcham Flat. The unnamed mountain confronting them, which we will hereafter designate Mt. 8422, was a formidable obstacle. But, it was a much easier route than the steep ridge route over to Mill Valley or Lost Cannon Canyon. The many steep, snow-filled ravines between Sonora Junction and Mill Valley would have been nearly impossible obstacles to overcome. That night they did not succeed in getting the howitzer into camp. The howitzer was left about halfway up the south face of Mt. 8422, and less than a mile from their camp in the saddle near the top of the mountain. "This was the most laborious day we had yet passed through, the steep ascents and deep snow exhausting both men and animals," Frémont said.

January 29. "From this height we could see, at a considerable distance below, yellow spots in the valley, which indicated that there was not much snow. (*Frémont was viewing Antelope Valley from an area on the west face of Mt. 8422, and near the peak. It is the only location in the area where he would have this particular view.*) One of these places we expected to reach tonight; and some time being required to bring up the gun, I went ahead with Mr. Fitzpatrick and a few men, leaving the camp to follow, in charge of Mr. Preuss. We followed a trail down a hollow where the Indians had descended, the snow being so deep that we never came near the ground; but this only made our descent the easier, and, when we reached a little affluent to the river at the bottom, we suddenly found ourselves in presence of eight or ten Indians. (*This "little affluent to the river" is not Deep Creek. Deep Creek is approximately one mile further north over another high ridge and down a steep and treacherous canyon. Frémont's trail down a gradual decline crosses a "little affluent," which is very difficult to see until you are in it. This twenty foot wide and ten foot deep little affluent is spring-fed about 300 yards above where Frémont used it to follow the trail down to the river.*) The Indians seemed to be watching our motions, and at first they were indisposed to let us approach, ranging themselves like birds on a fallen log on the hillside above our heads, where, being out of reach, they thought themselves safe. Our friendly demeanor reconciled them, and, when we got near enough, they immediately stretched out to us handfuls of pine nuts, which seemed an exercise of hospitality. We made them a few presents, and, telling us that their village was a few miles below, they went on to let their people know what we were. The principal stream still running through an impracticable canon, we ascended a very steep hill, which proved afterwards the last and fatal obstacle to our little howitzer, which was finally abandoned at this place. We passed through a small meadow a few miles below, crossing the river, which depth, swift current, and rock, made it difficult to ford; and, after a few more miles of very difficult trail, issued into a larger prairie bottom, at the farther end of which we encamped, in a position rendered strong by rocks and trees. (*This is the West Walker River and Canyon south of Coleville, California. This canyon, river, and valley description fits no other within ninety miles in any direction.*)

THE SITE OF FRÉMONT'S CAMP AT BRIDGEPORT
Viewing the Sierra Nevada to the West. The town of Bridgeport in the foreground.

DEVIL'S GATE
Looking west through the pass leading to the West Walker River and the approach to Mountain 8422.

BURCHAM FLAT
Looking north across the flat toward Mountain 8422.

THE SOUTH FACE OF MOUNTAIN 8422
The trail north up the mountain appears deceptively gradual —
with no hint of the difficulties to come.

THE SADDLE OF MOUNTAIN 8422
Frémont camped here on January 28, 1844.
The cannon was abandoned here or near here the next day.

THE NORTH FACE OF MOUNTAIN 8422
A steep drop-off to the left leads down to the West Walker River.
In the far distance is the Antelope Valley and the present-day town of Coleville.

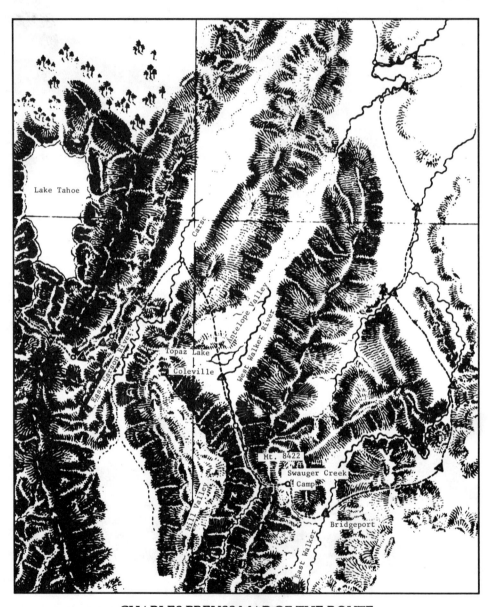

CHARLES PREUSS MAP OF THE ROUTE
A portion showing the section of the route near the Bridgeport area.
Preuss' map clearly shows the route following the West Walker River to Coleville.
Place names have been added for orientation.

From Frémont's *Report of the Exploring Expedition*, 1845.

Frémont continued, "The Indians brought in during the evening an abundant supply of pine nuts, which we traded from them. When roasted, their pleasant flavor made them an agreeable addition to our now scanty store of provisions, which were reduced to a very low ebb. Our principal stock was in peas, which it is not necessary to say contain scarcely any nutriment. We had still a little flour left, some coffee, and a quantity of sugar, which I reserved as a defense against starvation. The Indians informed us that at certain seasons they have fish in their waters, which we supposed to be salmon trout; for the remainder of the year they live upon the pine nuts, which form their great winter subsistence — a portion being always at hand, shut up in the natural storehouse of the cones. At present, they were presented to us as a whole people living upon this simple vegetable." *(This diet may explain why they were such a small and primitive race.)* The other division of the party did not come in to-night, but encamped in the upper meadow, and arrived the next morning. They had not succeeded in getting the howitzer beyond the place mentioned, and where it had been left by Mr. Preuss in obedience to my orders; and, in anticipation of the snow banks and snow fields still ahead, foreseeing the inevitable detention to which it would subject us, I reluctantly determined to leave it there for the time. It was of the kind invented by the French for the mountain part of their war in Algiers; and the distance it had come with us proved how well it was adapted to its purpose. We left it, to the great sorrow of the whole party, who were grieved to part with a companion which had made the whole distance from St. Louis, and commanded respect for us on some critical occasions, and which might be needed for the same purpose again. *(It is interesting to note that Preuss made no comment on being in charge of the cannon when it was abandoned. Because of his feelings toward the howitzer, it could be expected that he would have devoted considerable diary space to such an event. Not only did he not do so, he only mentions it casually eleven days later on February 8: "We had to abandon the cannon a few days ago.")*

John C. Frémont wrote this part of the narrative many months later. Upon his return to Washington, D.C., his wife, Jessie, and her father, Senator Benton, had told him of the concern he had caused with the requisition of the cannon. Acutely aware of the necessity of justifying his taking the cannon, its subsequent uses, and its final abandonment would and did require political and literary expertise. Although he was riding a crest of public popularity, the U.S. Army would insist on an explanation of the loss of a valuable piece of ordnance and nearly 500 pounds of powder and ammunition. This was not as difficult as it may appear, but it would have to be handled delicately and with finesse, and as accurately or nearly as accurately as possible. On one occasion he credited the cannon with preventing an Indian attack; this was politically sufficient in justifying its presence. A very steep hill rising from a deep canyon in an unknown region is also an appropriately rugged locale to abandon it. To further insulate his position, Frémont disassociated himself from the cannon. This is abnormal because from the beginning, he had insisted that the cannon spend each night in front of his teepee. Indeed, whenever the expedition was separated into two contingents he always took the cannon with his group. When it was abandoned on the 28th, he had not seen it since the camp on Swauger Creek or somewhere on Burcham Flat during the tortuous trek up Mt. 8422. All references to the cannon are spaced almost a page apart in the narrative; it is under the charge of another member of the party; it is always behind him; it is finally abandoned at his direction in a location impossible to traverse and when he is at least seven miles in front of its final resting place. It is also intriguing to note that he selected January 28 as the date to explain that his last chronometer was defective, and thus implying no longitudes would be recorded from that day on. Actually, the chronometer was probably broken in mid-December, because no longitudes were recorded between December 14 and

February 14. And he later commented that the two recorded February longitudes were only estimates. He resumed recording longitudes March 25, after leaving Sacramento.

All these points may or may not be relevant, but they are politically and bureaucratically expedient. They are not logical. It should be reaffirmed that a near truth about the unknown is as effective as the absolute truth. Any subsequent accusations or insinuations of discrepancy are easily explained as slight miscalculations or minor irregularities, and if a subordinate is temporarily in charge, the responsibility can be blamed on him.

Of particular interest is that on its final day and perhaps for the only time, Frémont said that the cannon was left in charge of the man who hated it the most, Charles Preuss. This had to be intentional. Because of his many critical comments in his diary, Preuss' feelings of hate for the cannon could not have been hidden from Frémont for so many months. It may have been a gesture of some sort from Frémont to the morose and unhappy Preuss. Whatever Frémont's reasons, they were unusual.

A series of subsequent incidents would further cause some historians to misinterpret Frémont's route from Fales Hot Springs to Antelope Valley. Because of a few newspaper articles written between 1859 and 1864, plus unverified stories from the early settlers of Antelope and Mill valleys, the weapon was thought to have been found by a man named Sheldon. The general belief was that he had found it among a group of abandoned emigrant wagons near Mill Valley in July 1861.

Mill Valley is a serene and beautiful valley that parallels the West Walker River Canyon to the west. The valley is separated from the canyon and river by a high, steep jagged sawtooth mountain. In the 1880's a government geographical party came in to survey the area. Early settlers who had come to Antelope Valley in 1859 may have told them the local legend of the cannon's discovery, which probably caused the survey party to name Lost Cannon Peak and Lost Cannon Creek. They also surmised that since Frémont had commented on his intention to continue down the valley from Fales Hot Springs, he had done so. While drawing their maps, they commented that his route was down Hot Springs Creek to the Little Walker River and up and over the steep barrier ridge to Mill Valley and then down to Antelope Valley. This was forty years after the cannon was abandoned and it all seemed simple- Sheldon had taken the "Frémont Cannon" to Virginia City, Nevada, sold it, and supposedly it had been prominently displayed there. The mapped route seemed logical, caused no concern, and for all intents and purposes, no questions were raised for another thirty years. Frémont's biographers, interested in the total man and the seventy-seven years of his fascinating and very full life, found these few days and the loss of the cannon to be only a minor incident and consequence. This is understandable, and in this adventurous life a true and accurate determination. The public's acceptance of the Sheldon cannon as Frémont's, the non-interest in the mistaken route of Frémont's trail, and the passage of nearly a century were the fortunate series of events that preserved this historical artifact in its hiding place.

Frémont's route from Fales Hot Springs to Antelope Valley can be accurately determined:

1. Photo enlargements of the Frémont-Preuss maps of the area clearly show the route of the expedition to be across Burcham Flat and east of the West Walker River until they are well past Mt. 8422 and further down the canyon. Significantly, the Mill Valley area and the rivers, mountains, and creeks of the area are clearly depicted as the route not used. [See map.]

2. Despite the one comment about his "intent" to follow Hot Springs Creek, all landmarks mentioned in the narrative are on the Burcham Flat-Mt. 8422 route. None are on the Mill Valley route. And, this comment was written about one year later.

3. A walking examination of the entire area shows there was no other reasonable route to the north.

As Frémont stated, January 28, 1844, was a most laborious day. Leaving their camp on Swauger Creek the party wearily trudged through Devil's Gate and passed Fales Hot Springs. Trying to reach Burcham Flat too quickly, they turned north into a series of steep embankments that nearly exhausted the men and animals, but after criss-crossing the exposed ridges to avoid the snow drifts in the depressions, they reached the south end of the Flat early in the afternoon. After rest and a meager lunch, they crossed the sagebrush covered plain three miles to Little Burcham Creek. The party with the cannon fell behind because of snow and thickly bunched, wire-like sagebrush. A healthy artemisia (sagebrush) plant is a formidable obstacle for mules to pull a half-ton of cannon, carriage, and ammunition through, over or around. It is normal for a man or animal to walk twenty to thirty yards around, rather than ten yards straight ahead over these spiny bushes which often are as tough as a roll of barbed wire. They arrived at Burcham Creek about 4 p.m., when Frémont and most of the party were probably setting up camp in the saddle of the mountain 1000 feet above and one mile in front of them. By nightfall, the cannon party was about halfway up the south face of the mountain when they unhitched the mules, left the cannon, and rode on up to the camp.

The next morning, while the cannon party was going back down the south face of Mt. 8422 to retrieve the howitzer, Frémont, Fitzpatrick, and a few others rode down the north face of the mountain along a rough but gradual trail to the river. As he talked with a group of Washoe Indians, Frémont looked around at the rugged ice and snow covered canyon. Knowing the cannon could go no farther, he sent a messenger, probably Kit Carson, back to the camp with this welcome news. The courier probably arrived in camp at about the same time as the cannon party returned with the cannon. It was a jubilant group that rode away from the little howitzer, sitting atop its carriage in a small meadow on this high, wind-swept mountain on the edge of the Sierra Nevada. They may have tried to cache the 500 pounds of ammunition, but they probably made no attempt to conceal or dismantle the cannon. They just rode away.

Why did Frémont requisition and take the cannon with him on an expedition entirely scientific in nature? Generations of historians have and still do take literary pot-shots at Frémont for this not insignificant incident. Numerous accusations have been made, everything from ingenious international plots to Frémont's delusions of grandeur. The most usual criticism was that it was totally unnecessary to the expedition. Frémont's stated reason for taking the cannon was that it was needed for defense against hostile Indians. This certainly could have been true. Frémont had been given quite a scare by marauding Indians at Fort Laramie just one year earlier. He undoubtedly had heard of traders William Sublette, William Becknell and others who had made very effective use of small cannons to protect their wagon trains of merchandise. He also knew that units of the First Dragoons wouldn't think of starting a campaign without their howitzers.

Somehow he heard of this older model French howitzer at the St. Louis Arsenal. He may have even seen it a number of times between 1838 and 1843. Because he requested the howitzer only one or two days before leaving on the expedition, some historians have read mystery and subterfuge into this. More probably, considering Frémont's impetuous nature, the thought struck him and he quickly acted on it.

As a "fait accompli," Frémont claimed only one incident where the howitzer played a decisive role and saved the expedition from an Indian attack. This was while in camp in the valley of the North Fork of the Platte River, August 5, 1843. He hinted at its deterrent capability on another occasion. Interestingly, when the ten men he sent back from Fort Hall arrived in St. Louis, in newspaper interviews, to a man they all claimed the howitzer was the only thing that saved them from the attack at the Platte River camp. The reason they were asked was because the howitzer had become a political issue. This was, of course, unknown to Frémont at the time. By November 1843, it was public knowledge that the War Department had refused to sanction Frémont's taking the cannon. Press leaks were as common then as now. Senator Benton was very upset and found that the "leak" came directly from Acting Secretary of War, James Madison Porter. On December 29, 1843, when Porter's appointment came before the Senate, Benton led the opposition and Porter's nomination was rejected by a vote of 38-3. Senator Benton was a very powerful politician and often brutally vindictive.

It has often been asserted that Frémont also disobeyed orders when he returned by way of California. This is rather ridiculous because his orders did not include a return route. In the first plan submitted to the war department, the expedition intended to return by the headwaters of the Missouri River. Later, probably in early April 1843, inter-department correspondence indicates the headwaters of the Arkansas River as the route of return. The Arkansas River route was much more desirable because of the heated border disputes with Mexico and Texas. Apparently during this expedition, as with earlier ones, only the main objective of the survey was in the written order. The return route was the province and responsibility of Frémont.

Frémont's epic, but near disastrous crossing of the Sierra Nevada in mid-winter has inspired hours of discussion and reams of written comment, pro and con. As far as we know, he only considered two plans. His intended route of return was through Nevada, Utah, Colorado and the headwaters of the Arkansas and Bent's Fort. This was probably impossible on January 18, or 26, whenever he abandoned this plan. His animals were foot-sore and breaking down. Some were dying and some were being stolen and there was no place to find fresh healthy animals between his camp and Bent's Fort. The winter of 1843-44 was bitter cold in the Sierra, but the snowfall was relatively light. Historically, light snowfall in the Sierra usually means heavy snowfall in the Rockies. Even had he turned back up the Humboldt and gone back by way of Fort Hall, South Pass and Fort Laramie, it would have been a trek equal in difficulty and much longer than his final decision — his historic crossing of the central Sierra via Carson Pass to New Helvetia.

As previously mentioned, there was a third alternative apparently never considered. Why didn't he return to Truckee Meadows for a couple of months? He could have easily lived on the Cutthroat trout and other game in the area. There was excellent forage for his animals. And, well-rested they could have resumed their journey east along the intended route in early March or crossed the Sierra by Donner, Yuba or Henness passes in late March or early April. Either would have been preferable to the Sierra crossing in February. He would have saved the cannon, about seventy horses and mules, nine of his men and he wouldn't have subjected himself and the others to indescribable suffering. But success explains or excuses almost any mistake, especially in such a geographical and political climate. The cannon was abandoned, Frémont's desperate men were generously attended to by General Sutter, and his return did not go near or otherwise alarm Mexican officials. He steered well clear of Los Angeles and Santa Fe.

Impetuous, daring men such as Frémont inevitably extend themselves too far. A calculated risk does not include foolhardiness. Frémont did not understand that there are mountains too high, deserts too dry and places too far. Such men are to an extent self-destructive. They do not comprehend that others upon whom they must depend may not have their courage, determination or stamina. He was to commit this "sin" many times in his life and it would always prevent him from reaching the lofty pinnacles he sought to reach.

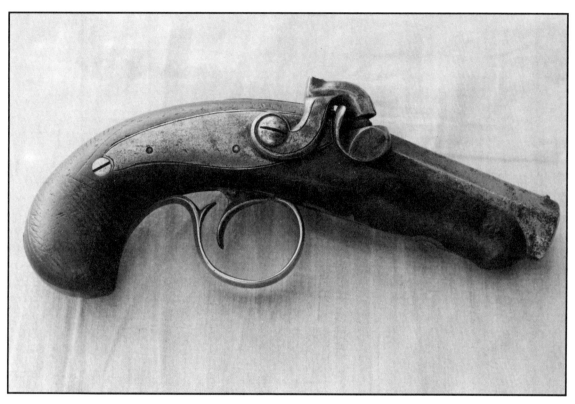

This Deringer was found in the early 1850's by Dan Hawkins at Fremont's camp area west of Markleville, CA
Nevada State Museum - Photo by Walt Mulcahy

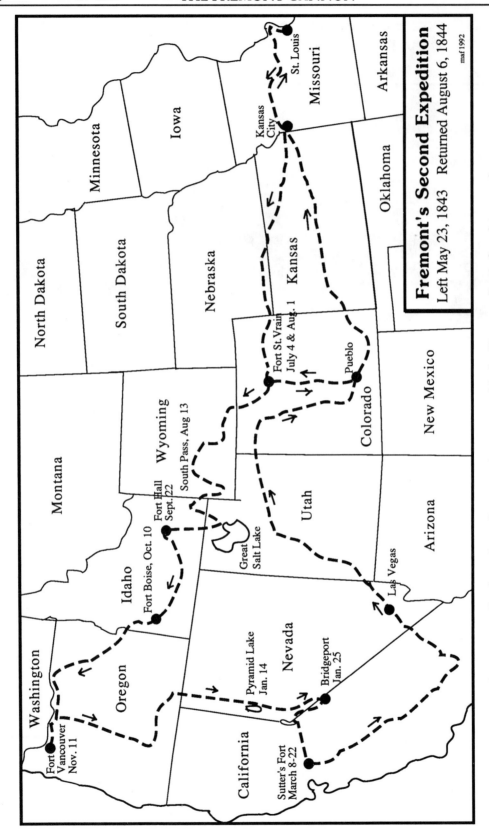

Fremont's Second Expedition
Left May 23, 1843   Returned August 6, 1844

maf 1992

The cannon, fired on about five occasions, was with the Fremont Party for nine months and traveled over 3,900 miles before it was abandoned, just beyond Bridgeport, California.

Chapter V

THE NEVADA MUSEUM CANNON

THE BRONZE twelve-pound mountain howitzer in the Nevada Museum at Carson City has a fascinating history, and for well over a century it was believed to be Frémont's lost cannon. It is distinctive in that it is one of the first bronze artillery pieces manufactured in the United States, and it is almost certainly the cannon General Kearny lost at the Battle of San Pasqual. It is not the cannon Frémont abandoned in the Sierra.

In the first half-century of the existence of the United States, most Army and Navy heavy guns were either purchased from other nations or captured in battle. Some found their way into U.S. arsenals as gifts from sympathetic allies. In the late 1820s, the U.S. Government recognized that this was an undesirable situation for an emerging nation, and initiated a program to manufacture its own cannons and other heavy weapons. In 1834, a private foundry, Cyrus Alger and Company of South Boston, Massachusetts, was selected to manufacture gun-metal bronze cannons. After considerable experimentation with the improvement of alloys and their proportions, the project was completed in early 1836. In June of that year, the U.S. Army was satisfied with the product and ordered a dozen twelve-pound mountain howitzers. The tubes were delivered in May 1837, and shortly thereafter outfitted with carriages and caissons at Watervliet Arsenal, West Troy, New York. The cost was $225 each. The third howitzer cast of these original twelve, and the only known survivor, is the cannon in the Nevada Museum. (*This is a short summary and perhaps an over simplification of a very difficult project. And the researcher's task in delving through mountains of army and congressional records was no less difficult. This short summary is provided from lengthy and thorough investigations by Carl P. Russell and Fred I. Green. Copies of their letters and substantive evidence of the officials involved, the contracts negotiated, and how the plans were obtained are available and can be purchased from the Nevada Museum. Recently, the author found another Cyrus Alger twelve-pound mountain howitzer in the museum at Fort Union, N.M. It may be one of the 1845 models. There is another later model 12-pound mountain howitzer in the Ft. Garland, Co., Museum. Bronze is an alloy of tin and copper. The Cyrus Alger bronze howitzers were approximately ninety percent copper and ten percent tin. Brass cannons were made of an alloy of zinc and copper. Carl P. Russell, author of* Guns of the Early Frontier, *revised his findings some years later when he questioned his original research on how many howitzers were made and who made them. He thought he had found contractual evidence that Cyrus Alger & Company had produced and delivered thirty-six howitzers during 1836-38. Subsequently, he and Fred Green found evidence that these tubes were delivered some years later, in 1845. Since forty-three howitzer carriages were built and delivered and monies were appropriated by Congress for the purchase of cannons in 1837-40, it was their conclusion that 31 of the howitzers were of foreign manufacture.*)

During the course of the project to manufacture these weapons, monetary limitations, extensive experimentation, and accidents convinced officials that the bronze cannon tubes were the most fundamentally sound. Lt. Col. George Talcott, assistant to the commander of the U.S. Army Ordnance Department, was in charge of the project and made the decision. In 1847, Talcott wrote a brief but interesting history of American cannons. He noted that brass cannons were not acceptable because of their excessive cost. And their battle durability was suspect. Unexpected bursting of iron field guns further cemented his commitment to "the Talcott bronze system of ordinance."

Tracing the early years of the Nevada Museum cannon is difficult to do with any degree of certainty. It is known that in 1837 one or more of the original twelve guns were assigned to the First Dragoons based at Fort Leavenworth, Kansas. Two or three others may have been stored at the St. Louis Arsenal. Near the end of the Florida Seminole Indian War when Jefferson Barracks, outside St. Louis, regained importance as a military post, one or two cannons were probably sent there. Perhaps thirty-one additional howitzers were bought by the Army before 1840, but most of these were assigned to the soldiers fighting Creek Indians in Georgia and Seminoles in Florida. (*Otis E. Young, The West of Philip St. George Cooke, 1809-1895, (1955). This book is not only a biography of Gen. Cooke, but also an excellent history of the United States Cavalry. The dragoons were cavalrymen who carried their own artillery. Dragoon regiments are often mistakenly identified as miniature armies in equipment and battle tactics because in their frontier years they were often accompanied by infantry companies. There also emerged in the early 1840s mounted infantry companies, but their battle tactics differed from the dragoons. The mounted infantrymen rode to the scene of the battle, dismounted and fought on foot. The basic dragoon battle philosophy was the cavalry charge where hundreds of rifle-shooting, saber-slashing men riding 1000-pound horses could cut a devastating swath through a mounted or unmounted enemy. Cavalrymen did not consider themselves effective when dismounted and this often was proved true; Custer's defeat at the Little Big Horn being the most noteworthy example. Some of the misinterpretation comes from the original congressional action which authorized and funded a mounted army unit on June 18, 1832. It was called, "The Mounted Infantry Bill," and called for a battalion of six companies of mounted rangers. However, this group proved to be ineffective and in December of 1832, the President signed a bill introduced by Richard M. Johnson, authorizing the formation of the First Dragoon Regiment. The regiment was to have 1,832 men and was subsequently organized as the "elite" regiment of the U.S. Army. Prospective troopers were told "it would be a disgrace for a dragoon even to speak with an infantry soldier." In 1837, the Second Dragoon Regiment was formed and by the early 1840s, after suffering through ten years of formative growing pains, the dragoons were in fact the most effective force in the U.S. Army. For nearly two decades their thin but proud ranks performed monumental feats of daring and courage wherever they were assigned and whatever their duty on the western frontier. Their leadership was exceptional and most of their officers of the 1840s and 1850s became generals during the Civil War. Emotional ceremonies at many military posts throughout the West decommissioned the regiments in August 1861. Thereafter they were called cavalry regiments.*)*

By any measurement, the new Cyrus Alger howitzer was highly successful and a valuable weapon in any command. Maneuverable, easy to transport, and deadly in its effect on an enemy, no commander would relinquish such a cannon without a critical or justifiable reason. On the other hand, an older foreign-made howitzer, perhaps not as dependable and without the newly developed methods of dismantling, might reasonably be assigned to a scientific expedition endorsed by powerful politicians. It was in such an atmosphere that Colonel S. W. Kearny allowed Frémont to requisition a brass (not bronze) twelve-pound mountain howitzer of the type invented by the French, not of the type manufactured by the United States. It is evident that the French howitzer inspired the U.S. model. It is also evident that the U.S. used different alloys, different carriages and developed a superior method of dismantling and transport. Unfortunately, the French Army Museum in Paris does not have an example of their twelve-pound mountain howitzer of that era. And they have been unable to locate any plans, pictures or sketches that might have survived the years.

For the first twenty-five years of its life, the Nevada Museum cannon must have had an exciting and adventurous time. It was probably with the 1st Dragoons on the western frontier, in California during the Mexican War, and was probably a sentinel over many famous and legendary forts. Wherever it traveled, it crossed a turbulent land in an adventurous era. It is almost certain that by July 1860, the cannon was at Fort Churchill, Nevada.

Fort Churchill was constructed on the Carson River about twenty-seven miles east of Carson City, Nevada, following the panic that swept through the area in the spring of 1860. Paiute Indians, rebelling against white atrocities, went on the warpath, burning and killing at stations along the emigrant and Pony Express trails. From a few adobe buildings in July 1860, Fort Churchill grew to a large frontier fort, garrisoned by 700 soldiers in the following year. With the advent of the Civil War most of the regular army units were transferred back to the States. Volunteers from California and Nevada took over the fort's duties in October and November of 1861. After the war the fort's responsibilities decreased dramatically. With the coming of the railroad, the telegraph, statehood, thousands of settlers, and the pacification of the Paiutes, the fort was eventually abandoned and fell into disrepair. It was sold at public auction in 1871. Fred I. Green's research of the building of Fort Churchill and of its first officers and detachments, shows that three twelve-pound mountain howitzers were assigned to units at the fort in 1860. Company A of the First Dragoons had one of them, and two were assigned to detachments of Company H of the Third Artillery. (*These should not be confused with the three newer type howitzers assigned to Major McDermitt at Fort Churchill in 1864. Following a secessionist victory at the polls in Storey County, an alarmed Governor James W. Nye felt that it was necessary to arm loyal citizens. Subsequently, the three new twelve-pound howitzers were assigned, one each to home guards at Silver City, Gold Hill, and Virginia City, in the fall of 1864. In 1941, General J. H. White, in his report to the Governor, mistakenly identified these cannons with other field guns that came to Nevada in 1874.*)

When most of the regular army troops were hurriedly transferred back to Union forces in October and November of 1861, the cannons stayed at Fort Churchill. Volunteers (Zouaves) patrolled the emigrant routes and telegraph lines. Because gold and silver from the mines at Virginia City and Gold Hill were of great importance in financing the Union forces in the Civil War, the mining districts of the area were almost as important to the Union as Washington, D.C.

Fortunately, most of the citizens of Nevada were loyal to the Union, or at least sympathetic, and the revolutionary efforts of Confederate activists were reduced to demonstrations, armed threats, individual fights and an occasional shooting. The two most critical events that defeated the Confederate activists were Nevada's designation as a Territory of the United States, March 2, 1861, and its admission as the 36th state October 31, 1864. William Morris Stewart, Nevada's first U.S. Senator, provided the leadership and political expertise in both of these accomplishments. The rebel sympathizers had many occasions for parades and boasting in the early part of the war when the Southern armies were winning battle after battle.

An interesting mystery began in late 1861 when one of the three Fort Churchill howitzers was quietly removed and retired from military service to become a lakeside ornament at Glenbrook on the beautiful east shore of Lake Tahoe. It seems very unlikely that the U.S. Army would retire a perfectly good howitzer while involved in a desperate national struggle. The tale of how a volunteer officer came into possession of the cannon, how the cannon was damaged and thus rendered useless to the army, and how it was mistakenly identified as the lost Frémont cannon is a fascinating tale of investigative history.

The year 1861 was not a period of chaos or anarchy in Nevada, but it was a time of unrest and turmoil. Into this scene, up the slopes of Sun Mountain to Virginia City, came one of Fort Churchill's howitzers in the possession of Captain Augustine W. Pray. During the first week of June 1861, one-and-a-half months after the surrender of Fort Sumpter and the start of the Civil War, Captain Tredwell Moore and twenty Dragoons from Fort Churchill were ordered to confiscate all weapons in the possession of Confederate sympathizers. They searched homes and business offices in Carson City, Silver City, Gold Hill and Virginia City. While they had some success, most of the weapons were hidden. More importantly, while in Virginia City, Moore organized a zealous group of civilian militia known as "The Union Blues." One of their leaders was Captain A. W. Pray. (*Capt. A. W. Pray's christened name, Augustine, is going to surprise dozens of historians who for over a century have been calling him Augustus. Old legal documents for the original plans for the Lake Shore House and Pray's original Glenbrook land grant disclose that Capt. Pray always signed his legal name, Augustine W. Pray. He probably preferred to be called Augustus and told people that was his name.*)

It is almost certain that Pray and the other leaders of the Union Blues, including Captain Moore, were either Freemasons or members of the I.O.O.F., but more probably Masons. The oath taken by Masons to their brother Masons, to their country and to the Supreme Being is a bond seldom broken. Most ranking military officers and political and business leaders of this era were Masons. It was Captain Moore's duty to organize and arm loyal home guards and volunteers. When Captain Pray asked for the little howitzer, Moore was not only happy to give it to him, but possibly pleased as well that he could station the weapon among trusted Masonic brothers in a most volatile area of potential secessionist trouble. (*Fred Green's research into the history of Fort Churchill convinced him that Capt. Moore had given the cannon to Capt. Pray and the Union Blues, but he could never find the link that would bind the two in such a mutual situation of trust. The Masonic brotherhood of these men would have been such a bond.*)

Captain Pray (1820-1892) was a native of Maine and a former ship's captain who had come to Nevada in 1860. He built the first sawmill in Nevada at Glenbrook, on the beautiful east shore of Lake Tahoe, in 1860. Pray had considerable influence and stature in the area because he was a dedicated supporter of President Lincoln and a respected leader among Union sympathizers. Probably in late June or early July of 1861 the combination of Pray's influence, Confederate agitation, and the importance of the Comstock mines convinced Captain Moore to arm Pray's volunteers in Virginia City with the howitzer. Unfortunately, the Union Blues were inexperienced in the use of the howitzer and they were inclined to be overly patriotic in their exuberance and devotion to the Union cause.

Sometime between the receipt by Pray and his volunteers of the cannon, and December of 1861 when the cannon was removed to Glenbrook, the cannon was damaged by an overcharge of gun powder. The incident may have occurred in a training session, or perhaps when each home guard tried to outdo the others in cannonade welcoming ceremonies for the incoming Territorial Governor, James W. Nye. In any event, a bulged cannon is a highly dangerous weapon to those using it, and certainly of no further use to a military force, and we know that the twelve-pound howitzer was removed to Glenbrook by Captain Pray at the end of 1861.

Whatever the circumstances surrounding the bulging incident, the fact that volunteers had caused the damage may well have been an embarrassment to the Fort Churchill Officer(s) who gave it to them. After the bulge was reported, a small conspiracy probably developed between the military and political leaders of Virginia City. Captain Pray, they decided, would take possession of the howitzer as quickly and quietly as possible; the military at Fort Churchill would report the cannon bulged in a training exercise (a welcoming firing of the gun for Governor Nye could be classified as training); and most importantly, news stories would be planted that the little cannon was Frémont's and had been found where he abandoned it. The publishers of the Territorial Enterprise, Joe

Goodman and Dennis McCarthy, were dedicated Unionists and would have entered into this conspiracy spiritedly. As Lucius Beebe said, "The word journalist had no place in Virginia City. The right-thinking, forward-looking, and professional ethics to which modern newspaper publishers lay claim would have reduced Joe Goodman or Dennis McCarthy to inextinguishable laughter." After a few months, during which time the curious could visit and examine "Frémont's Cannon," Pray took the howitzer to Glenbrook. This is a reasonable solution to the mystery of how Pray came into possession of the Cyrus Alger howitzer and how he was able to move it to Glenbrook during the early years of the Civil War. To suggest that the Army would have allowed Pray to make a lakeside ornament of a perfectly good, highly effective and necessary piece of military equipment during a critical national emergency in a strategic location, is unthinkable. The howitzer had to be bulged and therefore considered worthless, before it left Virginia City. (*It has always been accepted without question that the howitzer was bulged sometime in the 1880s. The only written reference the author could find was in a letter from Ernest H. Pomin to Justice Clark Guild. Pomin wrote that the cannon had been bulged when fired in celebration of a wedding in 1887. Pomin wrote the letter when he was ninety years old and was recalling an event that supposedly occurred when he was eight or nine years old. It is very difficult to accept as historically accurate such a comment 80 years removed from the event.*)

Another singularly interesting area of concern is that the early western pioneers, settlers and gold seekers were avid admirers of a new art form — photography. Literally thousands of pictures have come down to us from the 1850's and 1860's. Thousands more have been lost, but it is indeed strange that no pictures of the Virginia City "Frémont Cannon" have been found. Hundreds of photographs of Virginia City and its inhabitants have survived the hazards of fire, cataclysm and time. None depict the cannon.

Captain Pray's bulged howitzer was pulled to Glenbrook on a carriage with high wheels, 36 to 38 inches in diameter, which he later removed and installed on a hay wagon. After removing the wheels, he mounted the cannon on a cement base about a thousand yards north of the Lake Shore House, an inn he built near his sawmill in the 1870's. Later he mounted it on a heavy wooden block and secured it with iron bands. Pray regarded the cannon as his, but as the years passed the community of Glenbrook commonly understood that it belonged to them. It was fired with blank quarter-charges on occasions of public celebration and patriotic observance.

After Captain Pray died in 1892, his widow reportedly sold the cannon to the Native Sons of Nevada about 1900. While it was being loaded onto a wagon, the teamster went into a nearby saloon. When he returned, the cannon had been stolen. For the next few years the gun was prominently displayed on Indian Rock above the commons at Tahoe City, California, on Lake Tahoe's north shore. (Whether this version or one of the many other versions of the cannon's movement to Tahoe City is correct, it was taken there.) In 1916 or 1917, a museum in California received title from the U.S. War Department for the cannon. The man with the order presented it to C. T. Bliss, William Bliss' uncle, at his office in the railroad station at the Tahoe Tavern, in Tahoe City. Someone in the next room overheard the conversation and when the man went to get the cannon it had disappeared again. For a time it was hidden in the storeroom at the tavern and later it was buried under the railroad shop at Tahoe City.

Because the cannon was bulged, it had been fired only on rare occasions for fear it might explode. Although Ernest H. Pomin insisted the last time the cannon was fired was at his wedding on October 2, 1901, he was probably mistaken because old-timers in Tahoe City recalled it being fired a number of times between 1900 and 1910. It was probably about this time, or a few years prior to 1917, that the cannon was spiked by driving a rattail file into the touch hole.

It is generally believed that Ernest Pomin was the man most likely to have had "possession" of the cannon between 1917 and 1938. Others knew where it was hidden, but none would reveal the location to an outsider. Pomin, the owner of Pomin's Tahoe Park Cottages, wrote Justice Clark J. Guild of the Nevada Supreme Court that he found the cannon wrapped in gunny sacks and hidden under the stairs of the Tahoe Tavern. Fearing it would be stolen or confiscated, he buried it under the floor of the railroad machine shop. Later, William Bliss, who wanted to return it to its former place at Glenbrook, asked Pomin to give him the cannon. Pomin, apparently wanting to rid himself of the cannon, gave it to him.

In the summer of 1941, Bliss presented the cannon to the Nevada State Museum as a gift. It was prominently displayed as "Frémont's lost cannon" when the museum opened on October 31, 1941. It is interesting to note in the correspondence between S. M. Wheeler, the first curator of the Nevada Museum, and William Bliss, that Bliss is clearly designated as the donor of the cannon. However, in subsequent correspondence and conversations with other interested people, Bliss mysteriously denies any knowledge of the cannon. He is especially careful to deny any implication that it was Frémont's lost cannon. In an interview with Carl P. Russell, Bliss did say that he was positive that the cannon had been brought to Glenbrook by Captain Pray in 1861. As earlier indicated, one of the major reasons Capt. Pray's cannon from Fort Churchill was mistaken for Frémont's was because of a few short newspaper articles. The first appeared in the San Andreas Independent in San Andreas, California, November 25, 1859: "A local man has recently returned from the Carson Valley and reports that two miners enroute from the Walker river to Genoa had discovered a small United States howitzer: It was just before crossing the spur of mountain that forms the southwestern boundary of Carson Valley. Its presence in that secluded quarter can only be accounted for upon the presumption that it is the gun mentioned in Lieutenant Frémont's narrative as having been abandoned by him in that neighborhood."

Although this article is at least third-hand reporting and makes no mention that the cannon was moved or could be moved by the miners, and the location is thirty miles over difficult terrain from where it was abandoned, it would indicate the possibility that the cannon had been seen. At least two other newspapers reprinted this article: the Mountain Democrat in Placerville, California, December 3, 1859; and the Los Angeles Star, Los Angeles, California, December 17, 1859.

The second and most often used and misquoted reference is the news article in the Daily Alta California published at San Francisco, California, July 6, 1861:

The Howitzer Abandoned by Frémont in 1843: "A man named Sheldon brought a brass howitzer, which he found on the east fork of Walker's river, to Carson City one day last week, and offered to dispose of it for $200. Failing to find a purchaser there he brought it up to Gold Hill. Some of our citizens hearing of its arrival, went down there with purchase money and nipped it before Gold Hill folks were aware of it. It will be used on the Fourth. There is quite a history connected with the cannon. Frémont, in 1843, when attempting to find a central pass across the Sierra, owing to the reduced state of his animals, was compelled to leave this howitzer. It always was an object of wonder to the Indians in that vicinity. They burnt the carriage and carried off most of the irons. but the cannon was too heavy for them to manage. Captain Truckee, the old Pah-Utah chief, had a wonderful idea of its power, and repeatedly requested the whites to go with him and get it. Old Peter Lassen, who was with Frémont at the time it was left, just before his death, tried to get up a party to go after it — *Virginia City Enterprise.*"

This is the article that has all the elements of a planted news story. The *Territorial Enterprise* reporter who wrote this seemingly hurried article shows some knowledge of the cannon, but makes a number of glaring errors which might not have been made if the reporter had more time to write it. Some thought the story was written by Dan DeQuille or Mark Twain, but this is not possible because they did not go to work for the Enterprise until 1862. It is puzzling why so many writers chose to use only those parts of the Alta California news article which suited their particular beliefs. They knew, or should have known, of the many errors in the article. As for the more flagrant mistakes: the year of abandonment is wrong, the general location of the find is twenty to thirty miles east of where the cannon was abandoned, Peter Lassen was not with Frémont, and the general content of the story is adventurous. It is also interesting that both Peter Lassen and Chief Truckee were dead when the article was written, which precluded them from refuting it. Unfortunately, the issue of *The Territorial Enterprise* from which this article was copied has not been found. The great fire of October 26, 1875, in Virginia City destroyed all the early copies of the newspaper (1860-1875) and those preserved today from that era have been found through other sources. Those that have been located are on microfilm at the Nevada Historical Society, Reno. Also, this news account coincides with Territorial Governor James W. Nye's arrival in Nevada, and the probable bulging of the cannon. It should also be noted that almost all the literate people in California and Nevada were well versed on Frémont's second expedition and the lost cannon. Many of them had used his narrative as a guide in crossing the frontier.

The next newspaper article appeared in 1864, in the *Woodland Democrat* of Woodland, California: (*"Frémont's Gun — A twelve-pound cannon was discovered in an unfrequented locality near Walker's river by a party of men and it was subsequently ascertained that it was a gun abandoned by John C. Frémont on one of his famous pathfinding expeditions when he ascended Walker's river into California to find a way across the Sierra Nevadas. It was brought to Virginia City and has ever since been in the possession of Young American Engine Company No. 2, who have furnished it with a new gun carriage at considerable expense. It was only used on rare occasions as firing salutes at daybreak on the Fourth of July, celebrating Federal victories, etc. The Provost Guard took it in charge yesterday and it is now at their quarters at the lower end of Union Street.*)

There are many possible explanations for this article, but the most likely is that a reporter for the *Woodland Democrat* was in Virginia City and telegraphed the story as it was told to him. It is also quite possible that the story was inspired by the cannon in Captain Pray's charge. And by this time both Dan DeQuille and Mark Twain were mischievous reporters on the *Territorial Enterprise* and often engaged in "putting on" anyone within reach.

Another article appeared in the *Virginia City Territorial Enterprise*, March 4, 1875: "*General John C. Frémont, the early explorer of all this region of the country, arrived here yesterday morning most unexpectedly ... We told him about the brass howitzer which we, in company with a half dozen prospectors found in the vicinity of Mono Lake in 1859, and which is now in this city.*" This article was written by Dan DeQuille and the cannon he mentions could not have been the cannon found by the two miners mentioned in the *San Andreas Independent*. Although in a similar time frame, 1859, the location is more than thirty miles south of where Frémont left it, and sixty miles from where the earlier 1859 discovery was reported. Neither could it have been the Sheldon cannon as the location is again thirty to forty miles from the Mono Lake region and not in the same time period. By this time, DeQuille was well-established as the editor of the *Territorial Enterprise* and his readers picked up each morning's paper to find out who had been skewered the day before. Perhaps DeQuille was just making conversation with the famous General, because in 1859, Virginia City was little more than a few hundred miners living in tents and working small claims. The "Rush to Washoe" did not begin until the spring of 1860.

Obviously, all of these newspaper accounts cannot be true, which makes them all suspect.

Since no artillery battles were fought in this region and Frémont abandoned only one cannon, these news articles and subsequent historical analyses and opinions are quoting questionable evidence as reference. It is quite possible all these news articles were written because of another howitzer — the Kearny-Frémont howitzer of the California rebellion. There can be little doubt that Virginia City at different times possessed and prominently displayed two or perhaps three howitzers during the Civil War years. Logic and the preponderance of evidence supports the conclusion that Captain Pray's cannon was the only survivor.

The first known historical questioning of Frémont's true route from Fales Hot Springs and the discovery of the cannon was published in 1911, sixty-seven years after the incident. James U. Smith, a native Nevadan and the son of pioneer Nevadan, Timothy B. Smith, wrote an article for the *Second Biennial Report of the Nevada Historical Society, 1909-1910.* Using Frémont's narrative as a guide, and a personal interview with one of the older settlers of Antelope Valley, it was Smith's opinion that the howitzer had been abandoned on the east side of the West Walker River eight or ten miles south of Coleville, California. He also believed the cannon had been found among abandoned emigrant wagons which were in Lost Cannon Canyon or another canyon near Pickle Meadows. Smith did not question or inquire into the authenticity of the cannon, which he thought was mounted at Tahoe City, on the north shore of Lake Tahoe. Smith's father, an early day rancher near Wellington, Nevada, said that he had seen the abandoned emigrant wagons in Lost Cannon Canyon in 1859. Richard G. Watkins, of Coleville, California, who had come to Antelope Valley in 1861, told Smith the cannon was found in one of the canyons leading to Sonora Pass from Pickle Meadows. It should be noted that both T. B. Smith and R. G. Watkins were very old men at the time of the interviews and were trying to recall the events of a half-century earlier, events which they could have easily read about in the newspaper or overheard in a hundred places. However, it was not unusual for emigrant trains to become lost in their eagerness to find shortcuts to California. Lost Cannon Canyon is a rugged defile which approximately parallels Mill Valley to the west, and is the second canyon west of the West Walker River Canyon. George Wharton James devoted a short chapter to Frémont's howitzer in *"The Lake of The Sky: Lake Tahoe,"* published in 1915. For the most part, James referred to Frémont's narrative, James U. Smith's article, Dan DeQuille (William Wright), editor of the Territorial Enterprise, and his own considerable personal knowledge of Captain Pray and the cannon's history at Lake Tahoe. James determined that Smith's version regarding the discovery of the cannon was correct, and it was his conclusion, based on his research, that Pray had brought the cannon to Lake Tahoe in 1861. In 1915, James states the cannon was on a hill overlooking the lake at Tahoe City. James was somewhat of a romanticist, but there are two significant items in his account: the little howitzer was at that time (1915) still mounted above the commons at Tahoe City, and he also had substantial evidence that the cannon had been brought to Glenbrook in 1861.

When Effie Mona Mack wrote her "History of Nevada" in 1936, she chose to combine the Smith version and research of a quarter-century earlier, and the *Alta California* news account of July 6, 1861, in order to present her own conclusions about the discovery and disposition of Frémont's cannon. Later, in 1965, when she co-authored with B. W. Sawyer, *Here is Nevada, A History of the State,* she had changed her mind and believed that the cannon had not been found. This is significant because Dr. Mack seldom changed her mind.

George and Bliss Hinkle tried to put all the pieces together in *Sierra Nevada Lakes,* in 1949. Although this book is well written and the historical documentation and their personal knowledge well presented, the premise again confuses historical interpretation. As with all writers who try to prove the Sheldon-Pray-Pomin-Bliss-Nevada Museum cannon is the

FREMONT IN THE 1840'S
From the author's collection.

CHARLES PREUSS
From *Century Magazine*, 1891.

PYRAMID LAKE AS SKETCHED BY PREUSS
The drawing cropped to highlight the cannon and geographical features.
From Frémont's *Report of the Exploring Expedition, 1845.*

PYRAMID LAKE TODAY
A photograph by the author from the same rock on which Charles Preuss probably sat
to sketch the drawing at left, on January 14, 1844.

THE NEVADA MUSEUM CANNON
A close comparison of this cannon, long purported to be that
abandoned by Frémont, with the Preuss sketch
at the left shows obvious differences in the two howitzers.

THE NEVADA MUSEUM CANNON, 1896
A photograph of the cannon on July 21, 1896, when it was fired in honor
of the launching of the *S.S. Tahoe* at Glenbrook, Nevada.

Courtesy of the Nevada State Museum.

Frémont howitzer, they become submerged in accounts written by others and once this tide engulfs the writer, he only adds to the confusion. The book is an example of an historian's primrose path. One of the greatest pitfalls awaiting the historical researcher is repetitive authority. More simply, one historian writes what he believes to be the truth; one or two generations later another historian quotes the first, et cetera and ad infinitum until the premise is accepted as truth without any justification other than questionable evidence offered by the first to explore the issue. And, each generation quotes and re-quotes the preceding generation in a problematical premise until it gradually becomes an historical fact … legend into history.

If just once during the years following the abandonment of Frémont's cannon and the acquiring of the other howitzer, someone would have said, "That is a very nice twelve-pound howitzer and I'm sure it has historical significance, but it doesn't appear anything like the cannon Frémont abandoned," perhaps not so much would have been written trying to prove that it was.

The only known "picture" of Frémont's cannon is the sketch Charles Preuss drew at Pyramid Lake only two weeks before the cannon was abandoned. Although Preuss' personality was occasionally criticized, his maps and sketches were highly praised for their accuracy and technique. Photographs taken from the location where Preuss sat to sketch the pyramid do not depict the scene as accurately as Preuss' sketch or the human eye sees it. A photo-enlargement of the cannon in Preuss' sketch depicts the howitzer as it was. There is no reasonable argument that the cannon appeared differently than the way Preuss sketched it. If the cannon tube including the handles was of a different type, if the wheels were larger, if the carriage was of a different configuration, he would have so drawn them. He depicted the cannon as it appeared to him, and because he sketched the pyramid, the lake, the rocky outcroppings, and the distant hills so accurately, it is only logical that his depiction of the cannon is also accurate.

THE FORT CHURCHILL CANNON - 1884
This photo was taken at the Lakeshore House Inn located on the southeast shore of Lake Tahoe, Nevada. It was owned at that time by Capt. Augustine Pray.
Nevada State Museum

AMMUNITION.

309. The ammunition for the mountain howitzer consists of *shells, spherical case shot,* and *canister* ; to all of which the cartridge is fixed by means of a *sabot.*
The charge of powder is uniformly eight ounces.
The cartridge bag is made of woollen stuff.

SHELLS, AND SPHERICAL CASE SHOT.

The shells, and spherical case shot are the same as for other pieces of the same calibre.
The fuzes are like those for field service, viz., the composition is contained in a paper case, which at the moment of firing, is inserted into a wooden plug previously driven into the fuze hole.
These fuzes being all of the same length, the time of burning is regulated by the proportions used in making the fuze composition. The two second fuzes are colored *black,* the three second *red,* and the four second *green.*
After the shell, or spherical case shot has been strapped to the sabot, it is charged with powder, the fuze plug is driven in, and the hole for the paper fuze reamed out. This hole is then stopped with a plug of tow, pressed in hard; the wooden plug should project about 0.1 of an inch from the fuze hole.
Charge of shell seven ounces rifle powder.
Charge of spherical case shot four and one-half ounces rifle powder, and seventy-eight musket bullets.

CANISTERS.

310. The canister for the mountain howitzer is filled with musket bullets; its dimensions and weight are as follows :

Number of bullets in each tier -	37
Number of tiers of bullets - -	4
Whole number of bullets - -	148
Height of finished canister, including sabot - - - - -	6.85 inches
Weight of finished canister, including sabot - - - - -	11.2 lbs.

FIXED AMMUNITION.

311. *Dimensions and weights of fixed ammunition.*

	Shell.	Spherical case shot.	Canisters.
	in.	in.	in.
Height of shell strapped, or canister with sabot	5.92	5.92	6.85
Height of round of fixed ammunition -	8.17	8.17	9.1
	lbs.	lbs.	lbs.
Weight of projectile, strapped and loaded	9.2	11	11.2
Weight of round of fixed ammunition -	9.8	11.6	11.8

CONTENTS OF EACH AMMUNITION CHEST.

312. The chest contains eight rounds of fixed ammunition, viz., two shells, five spherical case shot, and one canister.
Four of the spherical case shot are placed in the bottom tier, with the bullets down; the remaining spherical case shot, the shells, and the canister in the upper tier, with the cartridges down; the canister in the right hand end of the chest.

IMPLEMENTS, STORES, ETC.   85

In each chest are placed :

    4 two-second fuzes, (black.)
    7 three-second fuzes, (red.)
    3 four-second fuzes (green.)
    10 friction primers.

The fuzes and primers are wrapped in water proof paper, and the whole load well packed in tow.
A supply of friction primers, equal to half the number of rounds of ammunition belonging to the battery, should be carried in reserve.

WEIGHT OF PACKS.

	Weight.
313. The howitzer and the shafts of the carriage - - - - - -	250 lbs.
The carriage, with wheels and implements	295 "
Two ammunition chests, with the haversack, tube pouch, and fuze pouch, covered with the tarpaulin - - - -	238 "
Two forge chests - - - -	232 "
Two chests for carriage maker's tools (90 lbs.) with the coal sack (25 lbs.) - -	115 "
Saddle and harness, complete - -	53 "

The same kind of pack saddle serves for each of these packs.

RANGES.

314. *Ranges of Mountain howitzer.*

Charge.	Ball	Elevation.	Range.	REMARKS.
Pounds.	—	Degrees.	Yards.	
0.5	shell	0	170	
"	"	1	300	
"	"	2	392	
"	"	2 30'	500	Time, two seconds.
"	"	3	637	
"	"	4	785	Time, three seconds.
"	"	5	1005	
"	s. c. s.	0	150	
"	"	2 30'	450	Time, two seconds.
"	"	3	500	
"	"	4	700	Time, 2.7 seconds.
"	"	4 30'	800	Time, three seconds.
"	can'ter	4 to 5°	250	

315. *Table of Tangent scales for 12 pdr. Mountain howitzer.*

		Inches.	
Radius of base ring,		3.8	Point of suspension of the hausse 1 in. in rear of the base ring.
Dispart - - -		0.35	Distance to sight (radius) 33.91.
Tangent,	1° -	0.59	
	2° -	1.18	By dividing the space between the degrees, half and quarter degrees may be obtained.
	3° -	1.77	
	4° -	2.36	
	5° -	2.95	
	6° -	3.55	
	7° -	4.15	

MOUNTAIN HOWITZER AMMO, RANGES AND WEIGHTS
U.S. Army Mountain Artillery Annex - 1851

Chapter VI

WASHOE INDIANS VERSUS A FRENCH HOWITZER

THE SCENIC mountain country around Bridgeport, the seat of government for Mono County, California, abounds with cannon buffs in the same way that the shores of Loch Ness are populated by authorities on landlocked sea monsters. Almost everybody has a theory, even if they aren't all rabid enthusiasts. Most cannon buffs think the famous brass howitzer is still where Frémont left it in 1844, or at least close to that spot. All agree the Virginia City cannon of Augustine Pray was not the one abandoned by Frémont, but from there on speculation takes many twisting paths.

Some hearty souls pore over maps and historical journals, gauging hypothetical vectors from uncertain landmarks, and then trudge exhaustingly through the remote Walker River country. A few of these, a very few, go out repeatedly, year after year, as dedicated as Jason in his immortal quest for the Golden Fleece. Oddly, the more they search, unsuccessfully, the more convinced they become that the cannon is "there' if they only looked in the right place. They are not unlike prospectors from the west's fabled gold mining era in that respect, and sometimes the quest becomes a passion so intense that not even its desired culmination would result in complete fulfillment. There is considerable local folklore in Mono County about the cannon, stories of sightings and "lost" locations, and legends every bit as colorful as the people who tell them. Deer hunters have been a traditionally rich source of cannon tales. And fishermen, too, but the hunters somehow weave a closer fabric. Not one of these "leads" has ever produced the Frémont cannon, obviously, but some of the stories are convincing enough to arouse interest among even the most hard-bitten cynics. One account is worth repeating here because of the uncommon veracity of the people involved, and because there is logic in its substance.

Harry Tom, a Maidu-Paiute Indian, was a guide for hunters who came to Mono County seeking wild game. Tom was widely respected for his athletic ability, sagacity and honesty. In October of 1936, he was closely examining the old 1881 Irvin cannon in front of the Mono County Courthouse at Bridgeport, when Ella M. Cain stopped to talk with him. Ella asked why he was so interested in an old relic that he had walked by hundreds of times. Matter-of-factly he replied, "Oh, it looks a lot like the one I saw out in the mountains a few years ago." Mrs. Cain's interest was immediately piqued. At the time she was Mono County's foremost historian, a former school teacher, and perhaps the area's most respected lady. She was acutely aware of the history of the Frémont cannon and the many sagas and legends surrounding its mystique. She pressed Tom for more information: Where did he see the cannon? When? Was anyone with him? "It was the 1928 hunting season, I think," he said. "I was guiding some flatlanders, riding the low side of the hill trying to scare deer up to the hunters riding the ridge above me. About noon, I stopped to rest my horse and there it was — back in a brushy area in a thick little grove of trees. I kind of shoved my way in to take a good look at it." Tom further described the cannon's carriage as being in bad shape. One wheel was broken and the other almost buried. And, the wood was brittle and crumbly with age. "But, it sure looked a lot like this one," he said again.

"Did you ever tell anyone about it," Ella asked?

"Not that I remember, never had any reason to," Tom replied. Harry Tom's nickname was "Silent Tom," because he seldom had anything to say and, as was the nature of the time, he had few friends outside the Indian population. Ella's continued questioning of Harry Tom revealed that he wasn't too sure of the exact location because he and the hunters had covered a lot of ground in the days following. And, frankly, he hadn't given much thought to the cannon. He reminded Ella that with all of his other duties, such as setting up camp, caring for the horses, cooking meals, skinning the deer and bears killed, bagging and caring for the meat, breaking camp, and all the other jobs that go with his work, the cannon faded from his mind. It didn't seem that important. Tom did ask one favor of Ella, "please don't tell this to anyone but your husband. I don't want to be known as another 'drunk' who saw a cannon."

In the ensuing days when she would see him, Ella persisted in her efforts to jog Tom's memory. A few weeks later he came to her home and gave her a sketch of where he believed he saw the cannon. Because Tom was more interested in protecting his reputation as a responsible guide, he probably never knew the significance of his discovery. Ella took the little hand-drawn map given her and repeated her promise to Tom not to tell the story. It is relatively certain that she did not. Friends and acquaintances often asked her to tell the story, but she stood firm in her promise. (*This version is a composite of similar accounts told to the author by three men, Paul Jorgenson, Captain Clarence Brumbaugh, and W. Lee Symmonds. Symmonds was a renowned artist and was President of the Mono County Historical Society for many years. Capt. Brumbaugh was the Commander of the California Highway Patrol squad in Mono County for over thirty years, 1937-1968. Paul Jorgenson was an avid sportsman and CHP Officer who died tragically in a hunting accident in the early 1960s. All knew David V. and Ella M. Cain, and all three had a personal interest in Mono County history.*)

That winter of 1937 Ella Cain suffered a massive heart attack. Near death for many weeks, she subsequently recovered, but as with all coronary victims at that time she was required to rest and avoid physical exertion for many months. She never gave up hope that one day, she and her husband Victor, would follow Harry Tom's map into the mountains and retrieve the cannon. If they ever tried, they did not find the cannon. No one who knew them can recall either Ella or Victor making trips to the mountains. In fact, both were somewhat unique in the area in that neither of them were overly fond of the outdoors. Victor did occasionally like to fish, but that was about the extent of his sports activity.

As the years passed, Ella's interests were directed into more personally pleasing areas. A sprite, witty and competitive lady, she loved to play bridge. As often as she could get her club together they would play and afterwards she would keep everyone laughing with her stories of early day Bodie. Born in the heyday of this uproarious and wild mining town in 1882 she knew all the tales of the "Bad men from Bodie," and the bad women, too.

Her other consuming interests between 1940 and 1960 were the histories of Bodie and Mono County. She published her *"History of Bodie"* in 1956, and her *"History of Early Mono County"* in 1961. Ella M. Cain died in 1966, at the age of eighty-four. The little map to the cannon, drawn for her by Harry Tom, supposedly is still in a cardboard box among her effects. Where? No one seems to know.

The only time Mrs. Cain mentions the cannon is in chapter one of the Early Mono County history. She quickly passes over the subject, noting that it had not been found and was probably near Leavitt Meadow. In her own mind she was certain the cannon had not been found and Leavitt Meadows is an abstract enough location to be historically acceptable.

What did the Washoe Indians of Mill Valley and Antelope Valley do with the cannon after Frémont abandoned it? The tribe was a small aboriginal race of Indians and though surrounded by a plentiful nature, their lives were consumed by a daily struggle to feed and clothe themselves and their families. Compared to the Indians of the deserts only a few miles to the east, the Mill Valley and Antelope Valley Washoe lived in a paradise. Their staple food was the pinon pine nut which they ate in its natural form or ground into bread. Wild iris and flax grew in abundance from which they made baskets for hunting or fishing nets. Deer, antelope and hares were all around them, and the streams were full of fish. However, as Irene D. Paden wrote in 1943, the Indians of the Sierra were very small, scarcely over five feet, and very primitive.

A few historians have suggested that the Bridgeport Valley or Mono Lake Paiute may have had as much access to the cannon as the Washoe from Antelope Valley. Although this is a possibility, it is not a probability. The Indians Frémont talked with January 29, 1844, were almost certainly Washoe and not Paiute. They accompanied Frémont down the canyon to Antelope Valley and to their village. The Washoe did not have horses and could only have moved the cannon with muscle, if they moved it at all. The cannon and carriage weighed more than 500 pounds, Whether the cannon was left on Mt. 8422 or in West Walker Canyon, it would have been terribly difficult, perhaps impossible for these Indians to move the cannon a distance of more than a mile or two. This area is a maelstrom of obstacles to walk through, and to push or pull by hand a 500-pound wheeled vehicle in any direction for any distance would be almost out of the realm of reality.

The *Alta California* newspaper account that states the Indians burned the carriage for its iron probably is not true. The Mill Valley Washoe of 1844 were a stone age people and had no knowledge of the use of iron. Even if their primitive minds recognized that this metal might make good spear and arrowheads, they did not have the knowledge to forge a fire to a high enough temperature to do anything with it. There were also a number of explosive shells in the ammunition boxes, and had these been put in a fire the explosion would have killed anyone in the vicinity.

The suspicion that Frémont ordered the ammunition cached must be seriously considered. Digging a hole into the rocky frozen earth would not have been easy, but if there was a natural depression nearby that could have been covered with rocks, then such a cache might exist. Approximately 200 yards from their campsite of January 28, 1844, near the saddle below the summit of Mt. 8422, there is such a natural depression. It is at the edge of the sheer horseshoe cliff overlooking West Walker Canyon. And, it is interesting to note that none of the newspaper reports of finding the cannon mention anything about finding the ammunition.

Most of Frémont's biographers agree that he was a sensitive and moral man who had great respect for all life forms. On a few occasions he had to approve, even condone, the killing of enemies. But, throughout his life his respect and love for wild nature was remarkable for a man whose life was often threatened by hostile Indians and an often malevolent nature. Whether or not his men were successful in caching the ammunition, he might have felt obligated to warn the Indians not to allow fire near it. (*There are those who will insist that Frémont and Carson would have happily set a fire around the ammunition and invited the Indians to cook their meal on it. Then from a distance they would have humorously watched while the Indians were blown to pieces. There is no historical justification for such an opinion at this particular time in Frémont's life. Perhaps a year or two later he would have considered it, but not at this time.*) It is doubtful the Indians would have dismantled the cannon from the carriage. They had no reason to try and they could not have done it even if they had printed directions.

One convincing argument that the cannon was of foreign origin is that at no time did Frémont remove the barrel tube from the carriage during the long journey. If Frémont had the tools or the cannon could otherwise have been removed from the carriage and packed by a mule, he would have done so many times. Either Frémont did not have the capability of removing the cannon tube from its carriage or he did not have a pack-saddle for a mule to carry the tube. Because a pack-saddle would have been simple to improvise, it seems probable that he could not dismantle the cannon. If Frémont could not dismantle the cannon from the carriage, certainly the Indians could not. If Frémont had been issued a Cyrus Alger howitzer such as the one in the Carson City Museum, he would not have had to abandon the cannon, only the carriage.

In 1851, the U.S. Army issued an instruction manual for mountain artillery. This manual was prepared by a board of Army Officers in 1850 as an appendix to the 1845 manual of artillery instruction. Lieutenant Jesse Reno, for whom Reno, Nevada, is named, did most of the technical work in the manual. Although it was published seven years after   Frémont abandoned his howitzer, the manual shows how to remove the Cyrus Alger howitzer tube from the carriage and mount it on a mule for traversing difficult terrain. The procedure was simple and took only a short time.

Although there is no reason to believe that the Indians would want to destroy the howitzer, the possibility must be considered. If this primitive impulse did happen, the most immediate and accessible place to destroy it would have been the granite cliff less than 200 yards from where it was left at the January 28 campsite. They could have pushed the howitzer over this precipice and the carriage would have been crushed to pieces 500 feet below. The cannon tube might have been damaged to some extent. If this did occur, the cannon is probably still among the huge boulders below. This is one of the least accessible and untraveled areas in West Walker Canyon. (The author was never able to search this horseshoe.)

Some historians have suggested that the Indians might have given some religious symbolism to the cannon, but this is doubtful. It was more likely considered only an interesting curiosity left by the white men. Because it was within their tribal hunting boundaries, the Mill Valley Washoe might have developed a kind of pride of ownership for this very uncommon object. Possibly in the summer of 1844, they might have reached the conclusion that the cannon should be hidden from their neighboring tribes, whether friendly or hostile. This could serve many purposes, but most importantly it might insure Washoe ownership and if Frémont returned they would expect a reward for their care of the cannon.

The Washoe Indians of Mill Valley probably hid the cannon in the easiest manner in the least traveled area of their land, on the mountain where it was abandoned, Mt. 8422. They were limited physically, knew their normal trails, and knew that the mountain was the least frequented area in the surrounding territory by themselves as well as other wandering Indians from other tribes. This mountain is not attractive to hunters, fishermen or travelers, Indian or White. Pinon pines number in the thousands less than a mile to the north and west, but not on Mt. 8422. Sierra Nevada bears (including the grizzly, until the last was driven away in the 1920s), have lived on the mountain for hundreds of years. Until recently mountain lions still roamed the mountain because hunters did not often disturb them. Indians with bows and arrows were a poor match for bears and mountain lions, and long ago learned to live with this fact. The White man and his rifle changed things but not without many casualties. A number of Traders and Mountain Men were killed or injured by bears when they were careless or their first shot was not effective.

Bears and mountain lions will seldom attack a man if they are not cornered. Mountain ants will. There are millions of irritating, repulsive and infuriating ants on Mt. 8422. In the winter they are dormant, but when the snow melts they crawl everywhere. When a man stops to rest, or to study, or to observe the awesome scene around him, in minutes his legs will be crawling with large, loathsome, and viciously biting ants. It is not a pleasant place.

Within 500 yards of where the cannon was abandoned on Mt. 8422, Washoe Indians probably rolled or pushed the little howitzer to an overhanging ledge, or to a natural depression or rain washed gully. Within three or four hours they may have covered it with stones, earth and brush. Using sagebrush, they may even have brushed away the wheel marks. Then the Washoe went down the mountain, back to their valleys and continued their lives. In the ensuing years, before the prospectors and settlers came, they may have checked on the cannon when they remembered. But, gradually, as with all humans, the memory faded. When the settlers came to Mill Valley and Antelope Valley, and the miners came to dig in their mountains, the Washoe were steadily pushed out of their valley homes. Within a few years they were forced onto the reservations at Dresslerville, Walker Lake, or Yerington. The buried cannon was the least of their problems.

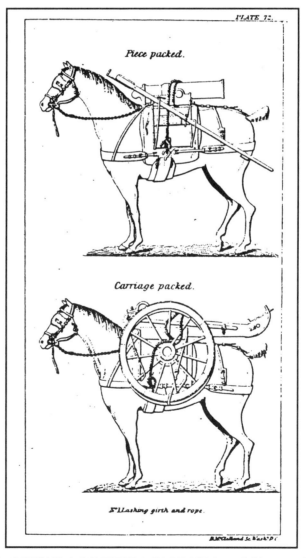

THE CYRUS ALGER - NEVADA MUSEUM CANNON could be easily dismanteled and packed. Fremont's cannon could not.
U.S. Army Mountain Artillery Annex - 1851

THE HORSESHOE CLIFF ON MOUNTAIN 8422
A view from the canyon bottom of the ridge over which the cannon
may have been pushed, and where it may still be hidden.

THE HORSESHOE CLIFF
This steep decline about 300 yards west of Frémont's camp of January 28
overlooks the West Walker River approximately 2200 feet below.

HARRY TOM, "CHIEF WHITE WING"
When this Maidu-Paiute Indian
claimed to have seen the "Frémont
Cannon" and described it, no one
ever doubted or questioned the
veracity of his claim.

Born in Yosemite about 1895, he
made a good living as a guide for
hunters, fishermen and mountain
enthusiasts. He was probably the
best athlete ever to live in Mono
County. A husky and wiry 5-foot-
five inches, he was a champion
bronc rider and rodeo performer
with an uncanny ability to train
horses and mules; the fastest runner
and longest jumper in all contests;
and an exceptional boxer. Indians
and Whites came for miles to watch
his war dances.

He died in 1979 in his beloved
Antelope Valley, and is buried in the
Indian Cemetery at Coleville.

*From the collection of Mr. and Mrs. Johnnie
Lundy of Bridgeport, CA.*

FRÉMONT AT 77 YEARS OF AGE
Harper's Weekly

Chapter VII

THE FRÉMONT-KEARNY CANNON

If the cannon in the Nevada Museum is not Frémont's, whose was it and is it historically important? Whoever appeals to authority reasons that something is true because some "expert" said it was true. Almost any field of history contains masses of material about which experts agree and they are happy to stay within the boundaries of their authority and expertise. But, there are some areas of history where authorities are few or non-existent, usually because historical documentation is lacking. When we place two or more similar objects together in order to measure their worth or establish identities, we are making a comparison. There is a considerable difference between stating a resemblance between two things and comparing two things. But, you can draw a conclusion from either a resemblance or a comparison. The sound practice of good reasoning comes from discovering and presenting relevant facts or probabilities that adequately support a reasonable conclusion.

There is another possibility, perhaps probability, which could connect and clarify many of the loose ends of this mystery. From the California Rebellion, only three years after Frémont abandoned his French twelve-pound howitzer on Mt. 8422, came a second much more highly publicized "Frémont cannon." This second twelve-pound howitzer is almost certainly the howitzer in the Nevada Museum at Carson City

In the middle of his third expedition, geographical circumstances and political events suddenly hurled Frémont from a highly qualified scientist-explorer to a poorly qualified soldier-conqueror and pivotal leader in the California Rebellion. The swirling, often uncontrolled events of the period placed him in the lofty position of Military Governor of California. The governorship certainly satisfied his ambitious nature, but in truth he did not have the training, experience or mature judgment necessary to cope with such responsibility.

Brigadier General Stephen Watts Kearny, the President's designated commander of the New Mexico and California military operations in the Mexican War had occupied New Mexico with little opposition. Intercepting dispatches carried by Kit Carson from Frémont and Stockton informing the President that California was conquered and at peace under the American Flag, Kearny continued on to California with only a token force of 100 dragoons, Companies C and K, First Dragoons, and two mountain howitzers. Unfortunately for Kearny, because of Stockton's and Gillespie's harsh policies, the Californios were neither peaceful nor conquered. Kearny was attacked and soundly defeated by Californios under General Andres Pico at San Pasqual in early December 1846. Kearny, seriously wounded himself, might have had his entire force annihilated were it not for the heroism of scouts who carried dispatches through enemy lines to Commodore Stockton at San Diego pleading for a relief force. During the battle, a detail of Gen. Pico's lancers lassoed one of the howitzers and carried it away. Five weeks later Frémont recovered the cannon when Gen. Pico surrendered to him at Cahuenga, January 13, 1847. (*This was Carson's version of how the cannon was lost and almost certainly the correct one. Gen. Kearny said that during the battle the mules pulling the cannon broke from their handlers and bolted toward enemy lines.*)

Archibald H. Gillespie, 1st Lieutenant, U.S. Marine Corps, is best remembered as the courageous and persevering secret agent who carried President James K. Polk's controversial messages to Consul Thomas O. Larkin and Frémont. The full context of these messages may never be known, but from them Frémont; rightly or wrongly, instigated and orchestrated the California Rebellion. Gillespie (1812-1873), after serving as Frémont's adjutant in the

California Battalion was appointed Military Governor of Southern California by Commodore Stockton following the relatively peaceful initial conquest. Although he was an excellent officer with a strong sense of duty, energy and initiative, he was viewed by the native Californians as a despot. In enforcing Stockton's regulations he was often too harsh and tactless. A blunt, outspoken and humorless man, he made few friends and many enemies. After his display of daring and courage at the battle of San Pasqual, his career steadily declined and he died in California in obscurity.

The battle of San Pasqual was fought in the beautiful valley about thirty-five miles northeast of San Diego on December 6, 1846. General Kearny pompously declared the battle a decisive victory, a false and vainglorious assertion. Kearny's men were nearly exhausted after the long march from New Mexico, but even on worn-out and poorly-fed horses they fought a spirited and courageous battle. However, they were out-ridden and confused by Pico's devastating use of his lancers and suffered at least three times the casualties as the Californios. Kearny lost twenty-two or twenty-three killed and at least thirteen wounded. After the battle they dug in on a strategic hill and waited four days for another attack. As the days passed, the position on "Mule Hill" became untenable. His men and animals tired and hungry, the painfully wounded Kearny decided on a desperate dash to San Diego. Fortunately, about one a.m., December 11, they were rescued by Stockton's relief force of sailors and marines. Had Kearny attempted his plan of escape, Pico's hard riding caballeros with their deadly lances would probably have cut them to pieces. The battle was not long, did not involve a great number of men and probably had little effect on the outcome of the war, but there was great courage and heroism displayed by the men of both sides.

Alex Godey, Thomas Burgess, and an Indian sheepherder carried the first dispatches from General Kearny, which Stockton acted on as soon as he could. Kearny, advised that all three were captured and thinking them unsuccessful, sent Kit Carson, Edward Beale and Che-muc-tah, an Indian scout, in a second attempt. (Godey and the others were captured, but on their way back from San Diego.) Although this second attempt was unnecessary the trek these men made was very hazardous and truly heroic as they ran, walked and crawled over the cactus, brush and rock covered mountains to get to San Diego. Carson and Beale spent weeks recovering from the ordeal.

In the turbulent months that followed, Frémont was caught between the conflict of authority that arose between General Kearny and Commodore Stockton. Foolishly, Frémont chose to recognize Stockton as the military commander of California instead of Kearny. Finally submitting to Kearny's authority after months of defying him, Frémont was ordered to follow at the rear of Kearny's column when they returned to the east over Donner Pass and back to the states. (This was in late June 1847, and the mutilated fragments of the Donner party dead were emerging from the Sierra snows when Kearny's party passed the site of this tragedy near Truckee, California. Kearny's column delayed a sufficient time to bury the remains.)

In late August, immediately upon their arrival at Fort Leavenworth, Kansas, Kearny ordered Frémont arrested for disobedience of orders. By the time he came to trial in Washington, D.C., November 2, 1847, army bigwigs had added mutiny and conduct unbecoming an officer to Kearny's charge. He was found guilty, following a lengthy and highly publicized trial, on all charges and specifications and sentenced to be dismissed from the service. President Polk confirmed the findings of the court, although noting he disagreed with the mutiny conviction, and offered to return Frémont to duty without loss of rank. Frémont refused and resigned because he thought he would be admitting guilt if he accepted the President's gesture. (It was a generous gesture indeed when it is noted, as Frémont did during the court martial, he could have been shot.)

One of the most intriguing aspects of Frémont's court martial was the lengthy day-after-day arguments, deliberations, charges and countercharges concerning the howitzer Kearny lost at San Pasqual and Frémont recovered at Cahuenga. Comparatively, Frémont's trial was as newsworthy and caused as much media attention during his time as the Scopes, Lindbergh or Hearst trials did in later years. The trial testimony was printed daily in the nation's newspapers and summarized in weekly or monthly magazines. On many of the days the testimony centered around the Frémont-Kearny howitzer - another Frémont cannon. This Frémont cannon became more famous and more widely known than the one he abandoned three years earlier on Mt. 8422. *(There were actually two howitzers surrendered to Frémont and both became embroiled in this controversy. For simplicity's sake and to avoid more confusion, the author has decided to refer only to the one identified by Pico as the one captured at San Pasqual.)*

People in California and other Western territories during this period were naturally starved for news of events in the east. Each new emigrant brought his personal bit of news, and newspapers and magazines came by the bundle in ship's cargo holds. They brought a premium price and were read, re-read and passed from person to person until they became shredded from use or the print became smudged and unreadable.

There can be little doubt that most people in California had some degree of awareness about the "Frémont-Kearny cannon" because it was notorious in the area many months before Frémont's court martial. In March 1847, it had caused considerable verbal and written conflict between Kearny's officers and Frémont's officers because Captain Dick Owens, one of Frémont's men, refused to surrender the captured howitzer to Kearny's representative, Lieutenant Colonel Philip St. George Cooke. Frémont issued Owens a written order not to relinquish any arms to any person without his personal directive. This act infuriated Cooke and he would forever be Frémont's implacable enemy. Eventually the howitzer was returned to Cooke and Company "C" of the 1st Dragoons while they were camped at San Gabriel. *(Cooke testified at Frémont's court martial that after the cannons were finally released to the 1st Dragoons, he took them to San Gabriel.)*

Lt. Col. Cooke testified, the Frémont-Kearny howitzer accompanied Kearny, Frémont and the 1st Dragoons to Monterey for the victory parade. It certainly did not go back to the states with them. Indications are that it stayed in Monterey with an artillery company and later when the artillery company was assigned to the Presidio at San Francisco, it went there to protect the entrance to San Francisco Bay. (Frémont spiked the ten Mexican cannons at the Presidio, July 1, 1846, early in the Rebellion.)

Naturally, this second Frémont cannon became a topic of controversy and conversation among members of Frémont's California Battalion, and certainly it was a topic of discussion among the regular army soldiers remaining in California. Nothing could be more logical than the soldiers at the Presidio pointing out to recruits or visitors their twelve-pound mountain howitzer as "Frémont's cannon." Especially when it again became so highly publicized during his court martial a few months later. The combination of so many prospective messengers, the mustered out California Battalion, newspaper and magazine coverage, and the massive "gold fever" army desertions of 1848, must have caused the cannon to be a topic of many discussions and arguments in the settlements and mines of California.

There is documented evidence that when Fort Churchill was established it was armed with three mountain howitzers sent from San Francisco. The author believes one of the three was the Frémont-Kearny cannon. The sequence of events thereafter is predictable. The two Frémont cannons became interchangeable in the minds of the people involved with them. The news events of 1847 and 1848 were no longer news in 1860. The gold bonanza, an Indian war and an approaching civil war were on most people's minds in Nevada. When one of the howitzers that came to Fort Churchill was identified as the Frémont cannon it was by this time only an interesting curiosity and its history undoubtedly somewhat jumbled. Settlers and miners in Virginia City, many of them having read and used Frémont's book as a guide in their trek to the west, could not be faulted for assuming the cannon was the one lost during Frémont's second expedition only about 100 miles south of their city. Probably none of the soldiers at Fort Churchill in 1860 were in the California Rebellion or at the Presidio in 1847, and mistakenly their Frémont cannon became the cannon lost in the snows of the Sierra. Logically, almost inevitably, the two cannons became confused and their separate identities lost.

The twelve-pound mountain howitzer in the Nevada Museum at Carson City is probably the cannon lost by General Kearny at San Pasqual and surrendered to Frémont at Cahunga. If true, it is a noteworthy historical artifact in its own right.

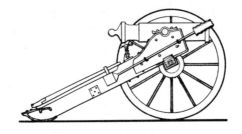

Chapter VIII

A LOST CANNON
IN SEARCH OF A FINDER

ABOUT one hundred million years ago the Sierra Nevada of California and the mountains of west central Nevada were injected with vast amounts of molten granite. Along with these intrusions from the earth's molten core came such minerals as gold, silver and copper. This material crystallized as a huge mass of solid rock. About twelve million years ago the range tilted up to a height of several thousand feet, and about one million years ago the final and greatest uplift took place, bringing the Sierra Nevada near its present height. Today these awesome, spectacularly beautiful mountains are home to thousands of people and a vacation paradise for millions, but in the 1850's the range was a treasure trove for the gold seeking argonaut.

Mt. 8422 has never been attractive to hunters, fishermen or other mountain sports enthusiasts. However, the gold and silver seekers of the gold rush era were a different breed. What kind of breed is perhaps impossible to define because in the rush to California's gold fields, men of every type and character were to be found. They were mostly young amateurs who had a consuming fever for easy riches. Most of them were also lusty and adventurous, and in that free and uninhibited environment developed an unusual capacity for liquor and gambling. Although the mountain where Frémont's cannon was abandoned appears to have no valuable mineral outcroppings, there can be little doubt that the early prospectors gave it some attention. How much and to what extent and over how many years is unknown. But with the Bodie Hills, Mono Lake area and the east slope of the Sweetwaters being productive over a lengthy period of time, probably very few prospectors spent any significant amount of time on this inhospitable mountain.

The Bodie Hills had the bonanza mines. The towns of Bodie, Aurora, Masonic and others had their mining booms and subsequent years of decline. As these mines played out and were abandoned, the miners moved down from the Bodie Hills across Bridgeport Valley and west into the Sweetwater Mountains. The major mining districts in this area were the Patterson, Cameron and Clinton belts on the east slope north of Bridgeport, and the Comstock belt along the crest of the range. Probably less than five million dollars was taken from the twenty to twenty-five mines that have operated in the area since 1878. Most of these mines have long since been abandoned and none are within miles of Mt. 8422, which is at the extreme western edge of the range. The Deep Creek mine, a very small operation which has not been worked in years, is about five miles north of Mt. 8422. Five miles to the south is another old mine. It ceased operations a few years ago and the buildings have been torn down. The highest peaks are Mt. Patterson, which rises to a height of 11,673 feet and Wheeler Peak, 11,664 feet. The Sweetwater range covers approximately 300 square miles.

The harsh physical reality of grubbing for gold and the stark economic reality of outrageous prices for food and equipment soon discouraged most of the miners. It was common for a man to work fourteen hours a day for one ounce of gold, or less. The elusive bonanza was always over the next hill or up the next ravine. One of the miner's favorite quotes, still heard today, was, "you never know if you are one foot from a million dollars or a million feet from one dollar." By the mid-1850's, most of the early argonauts were finding other jobs, opening businesses or returning to their homes in the east. The peak year was 1852, when an estimated 100,000 men swarmed over the rivers and streams of the western Sierra.

The early miners needed only a shovel and gold pan, but within a year or two they were using cradles and long toms. By 1852, they were using water-fed sluices, where a large crew could wash fifty to one hundred cubic yards of gold-bearing gravel in a day. During these years a fair percentage of the miners made a reasonable living. But, staying in the mines was like staying at a roulette table — the longer you sit, the better the chance you will leave broke. Many more prospectors ended up in other jobs than the very few who got rich. Ninty-nine percent of the dreams of El Dorado were just that — dreams.

As the placers played out on the western side of the Sierra, the prospectors worked east, up and over the summit and through the passes to seek the gold on the eastern escarpment and adjacent ranges. The Mono County mining chronology began with Lieutenant Tredwell Moore's Indian-fighting and trail-marking expedition of 1852-53. He brought back ore samples from Mono Lake to Frémont's Mariposa Ranch and showed them to Frémont and his miners. Moore also traversed Lost Cannon Canyon, Walker River Canyon and Sonora Pass, but made no report of finding abandoned emigrant wagons; nor were there any other indications in his report of miners or settlers in the area at that time.

LeRoy Vining crossed over the Sierra from Sonora and settled on Mono Lake about 1853 and probably discovered the first gold quartz in the area of Monoville in 1854. In 1857 a few hundred miners were working placers in Dogtown, a few miles south of Bridgeport, and in 1859 more hundreds were working the Monoville placers. The first Bodie diggings were discovered in the fall of 1859. The Bodie bonanza and rush did not occur until 1877, and between 1859 and 1877 little mining took place. Most of the miners moved on to more lucrative diggings. Mono County is an area of long, brutal winters. When the gold was not enough to keep the miners there, they hastily left.

Mono County, despite its hundreds of square miles, has probably never had a population of more than 12,000 people. In the 1880 census there were only sixty-four farms in the entire county. Also, according to the 1880 census, when all of Bodie's mines were in operation and at peak production, the Bodie population was not more than 10,000. By 1890, when most of the mines had been worked out, the census showed a county population of 2,002. The Mono County Clerk's office estimates the present-day population to be only 8,600, and many of these are part-time residents. Mountainous Alpine County, Mono County's northern neighbor, has a population of only 1,100.

The first farmers, ranchers, and townspeople started moving into Bridgeport Valley, Antelope Valley, and Monoville in the late 1850s and early 1860s. Stagecoach stations, roadside inns and other businesses sprang up along the roads leading from Mono County to Sonora over the mountains to the west, and to Genoa, Nevada, eighty-five miles to the north. But, in perspective, there has never been a great number of people in this vast mountainous area to intentionally search for or accidentally find Frémont's lost howitzer.

If this case was being put before a jury, the attorneys might present their closing arguments like this: the attorney supporting the proposition that the lost Frémont cannon was found and brought to Virginia City would recount that in the *Alta California* newspaper story of July 7, 1861, the cannon was indeed found on the East Walker River and that the basics of the article were true. He would also rely heavily on the newspaper accounts initiated by the article in the *San Andreas Independent* of November 25, 1859; the June 11, 1864 *Woodland Democrat* article again reporting the find; and the March 4, 1875, Virginia City *Territorial Enterprise* news story by Dan DeQuille referring to the cannon's discovery. He would also mention the few historians who believe the cannon was found because of James U. Smith's interviews with Timothy Smith and Richard Watkins. There would be little else he could present. Certainly he could not convincingly submit that the twelve-pound howitzer in the Nevada Museum was Frémont's. They are two distinctly different cannons.

The attorney representing those who believe the Frémont cannon is still lost somewhere near the West Walker River on or near Mt. 8422 would counter that the *Alta California* news article is replete with errors. It also coincides with the cannon being bulged and quietly moved to Glenbrook. He could also argue that this news story was intentionally planted by a conspiracy entered into by military and political leaders of Virginia City to cover up the misuse of a valuable military weapon. And, that this conspiracy resulted in the cannon's removal from a strategic military location to become a controversial ornament on the east shore of Lake Tahoe. He would explain the *San Andreas Independent* article as a news story written about two miners who may have seen the howitzer, but probably not in the area reported, and he would say there is no indication they moved it. He would counter the *Woodland Democrat* article with the assertion that the reporter was either repeating a story told to him, or he actually saw a different howitzer, perhaps one of the three newer types assigned to Fort Churchill in 1864. The attorney would refute the *Territorial Enterprise* article with a preponderance of evidence that the article had no basis in fact or truth. He would spend considerable time insisting that all the news articles were caused by the Frémont-Kearny cannon. The Smith interviews are not difficult to deal with when it is noted that both Watkins and Smith were very old men trying to recall events that occurred nearly a half-century earlier. It is also a fact that historians who have used these references were more interested in Frémont than the cannon.

The convincing evidence that the cannon has not been removed from the area would be presented after the above refutations. The sketch that Charles Preuss made of the cannon two weeks before it was abandoned clearly depicts that the appearance, configuration and carriage of Frémont's howitzer is markedly different from the museum howitzer. The cannon that Frémont abandoned was made of brass and of the type invented by the French; the cannon in the Nevada Museum is made of bronze and was made by an American manufacturer, the Cyrus Alger Company. Most historians and Frémont cannon searchers who have made in-depth investigations into this mystery believe the cannon has never been moved very far from where it was abandoned.

The Indians could not have moved it any significant distance, and probably did not burn or destroy the howitzer or its carriage. If they did anything with it, they probably hid it by covering it with brush, rocks and earth. The cannon was abandoned on one of the most forbidding, formidable and dangerous mountains in the area. Hunters avoid it, fishermen have no reason to visit it, and prospectors probably spent little time there. The entire investigation into the Sheldon-Pray-Pomin-Bliss-Nevada Museum cannon produces a much better case against its authenticity than for it. The attorney might also mention it is curious that no pictures have come down to us from the cannon's years in Virginia City. He would surely comment on the ten or twelve cannon sightings that cannot be authenticated, but noting that no one has been able to dispute the reliable sighting of Harry Tom and his subsequent story that convinced so eminent an historian as Ella M. Cain. And, he might conclude his case by noting that there is no real or physical evidence that the cannon was moved from where it was abandoned.

This story is not intended to be about John C. Frémont. Many very fine writers have done outstanding jobs in telling the story of his very eventful life. This story is about the little cannon he abandoned when his starving, exhausted force could carry it no further against the awesome escarpment of the eastern Sierra Nevada and its cold, windswept snow-drifts of mid-winter. Frémont, his wife Jessie, Kit Carson, Charles Preuss, Thomas Fitzpatrick and others have played their parts, but the central object and theme of this story is the cannon.

The locale is immense, the altitude steals the breath, the obstacles are formidable and the treasure is small. In winter it is bitterly cold and the deep snows belabor the human body and tire it in a short time. In summer the heat, rocks and sagebrush, and millions of ants mar the way and keep you from resting. Frémont's howitzer is still somewhere on Mt. 8422, or within one or two miles of it. It may be found this year or 100,000 years from now, but it is still there for those who don't mind a little discomfort while they take a walk ... high up and far back.

Advice and Counsel

The prospective cannon searcher should be cautioned about certain hazards and advised in other matters.

Persons with bad hearts, high blood pressure or poor muscle tone should not actively take part in a search because of the high altitude and treacherous terrain. The mountain's appearance is deceptive. Some areas are not difficult to walk, but a great physical effort is often necessary on most sections.

Do not use horses to search any part of Mt. 8422, except the south face. The east and west faces are obviously too steep for horses, but the north face appears to have a gentle slope that it does not. Steep rocky areas are hidden by thick brushy undergrowth. The author and his wife nearly killed themselves and their horses in this area.

Only experienced, well-conditioned climbers with the proper equipment should attempt to search the horseshoe on the west face. As mentioned in chapter six, the author has never attempted to physically search this area because he could never find a reasonably safe route in or out. Rattlesnakes have never been a problem on Mt. 8422, but to the west of the West Walker River over the saw-tooth ridges into Mill Valley there are substantial numbers of them. One family of black bears lives on the mountain in winter. The male is quite large and confrontations or territorial disputes should be avoided.

Bibliography

Bailey, Paul. *Walkara, Hawk of the Mountains.* 1954.

Bancroft, H.H. *The History of California.* VI. 1888.

Beebe, Lucius. *Comstock Commotion: The Story of the Territorial Enterprise.* 1954.

Benton, Thomas Hart. *Thirty Years View, 1820-1850.* 1856.

The Blue Book, California State Roster, 1893.

Bonner, T.D., ed. *The Life and Adventures of James P. Beckwourth.* 1856.

Brooks, George R., ed. *The Southwest Expedition of Jedediah S. Smith.* 1977.

Cain, Ella M. *The Story of Bodie.* 1956.

Cain, Ella M. *The Story of Early Mono County.* 1961.

Carter, Harvey Lewis. *Dear Old Kit: The Historical Christopher Carson.* 1968.

DeVoto, Bernard. *The Year of Decision, 1846.* 1943.

Egan, Ferol. *Frémont, Explorer for a Restless Nation.* 1977.

Frémont, Jessie Benton. "The Origin of the Frémont Explorations." *Century Magazine,* Vol. 41. 1891.

Frémont, John C. *Memoirs of My Life.* 1886.

Frémont, John C. *Report of The Exploring Expedition to The Rocky Mountains in the Year 1842, and to Oregon and Northern California in the Years 1843-44.* 1845.

The Frémont Court Martial. Sen. Doc. No. 33, 30th Congress, 1st Sess. 1848.

Garber, D.W. *Jedidiah Strong Smith, Fur Trader From Ohio.* 1973.

Hafen, Leroy R. *Broken Hand: The Life of Thomas Fitzpatrick, Mountain Man, Guide and Indian Agent.* Rev. ed. 1973.

Hammond, George P. *Alexander Barclay, Mountain Man.* 1971.

Hinkle, George and Bliss. *Sierra Nevada Lakes.* 1949.

Jackson, Donald and Mary Lee Spence. *The Expeditions of John Charles Frémont.* Vol. I. 1970.

James, George Wharton. *The Lake of The Sky.* 1915

Mack, Effie Mona. *Nevada: a History of the State.* 1935.

Mack, Effie Mona and Byrd Wall Sawyer. *Here Is Nevada.* 1965.

Marti, Wemer H. *Messenger of Destiny.* 1960.

Morgan, Dale. *Jedediah Smith and The Opening of The West.* 1953.

Morgan, Dale and Carl I. Wheat. *Jedediah Smith and His Maps of the American West.* 1954.

Mountain Artillery, U. S. Army Instruction Manual. 1851.

Neihardt, John G. *The Splendid Wayfaring.* 1920.

Nevada Historical Society. *Second Biennial Report, 1909-1910.* 1911.

Nevins, Allan. *Frémont, Pathmaker of the West.* 1939.

Nevada Museum (Carson City, Nevada). "Frémont Cannon Correspondence file."

Paden, Irene D. *The Wake of the Prairie Schooner.* 1943.

Preuss, Charles. *Exploring With Frémont.* Trans. and ed. by Edwin G. and Elizabeth K. Gudde. 1958.

Scott, E. B. *The Saga of Lake Tahoe.* Vol. 1. 1957.

Senate Doc. 14, 28th Cong., 1st Sess., Serial 432.

Stover, Tracy I. and Robert L. Usinger. *Sierra Nevada Natural History.* 1963.

Sullivan, Maurice S. *The Travels of Jedediah Smith.* 1934.

Talbot, Theodore. *Soldier In The West: Letters of . . . During His Services in California, Mexico, and Oregon, 1845-53.* Ed. by Robert V. Hine and Savoie Lottinville. 1972.

Talbot, Theodore. *Talbot's Journals.* Ed. by Charles Carey, 1931.

Wedertz, Frank S. *Mono Diggings.* 1978.

Wilkes, Lt. Charles., U. S. Navy. *Narrative of the United States Exploring Expedition, 1838 to 1842.* Vol. V. 1845.

Young, Otis E. *The West of Philip St. George Cooke.* 1955.

Financial Records,
1 Jan. 1843 - Dec. 1844

Editorial note: Because of sheer numbers, vouchers for the period after 1 Jan. 1843 will not be handled as single documents, but will be presented in summary form with the appropriate notes keyed to the voucher numbers. Several of the accounts for the second expedition were actually paid by Capt. Thomas J. Cram of the Topographical Engineers at St. Louis, although Frémont, who had returned to Washington, furnished the requisite funds and Thomas Fitzpatrick helped with arrangements (see William Henry Swift to Cram, 2 Sept. 1844, and Abert to Cram, 24 Sept. 1844. Lbk, DNA-77, LS, 7:391, 432).

The abstract of disbursements for the quarter ending 31 March 1843 is to be found in DNA-217, Third Auditor's Reports and Accounts, Account No. 16962. The abstracts of disbursements for the remaining quarters plus individual vouchers, statements of differences, and explanations for questioned disbursements are all to be found on Roll 1 of DNA microfilm T-135, a special consolidated file of JCF's accounts relating to his expeditions and the California Battalion. Those pertinent to this period are to be found under two categories, one of which is too narrowly entitled "Claims and Acknowledgments of Payments, 1842–1845, for the First Expedition" and the second, "Quarterly Abstracts of Disbursements, 1843–45."

Unless otherwise noted, all payments were made at the locale of the business firm or at St. Louis.

The editors have added the † and the * to the original documents.

The † indicates that the seller became or was a member of the expedition. The * indicates that Theodore Talbot certified that the property was "destroyed, injured, lost, & c." during the expedition. Talbot further certified that of the 224 head of horses and mules purchased for the use of the expedition, 163 were eaten, gave out on the road, died, or were lost or stolen. The remaining 61 were left on the frontier near Westport, Mo.

Abstract of Disbursements on Account of Surveys West of the Mississippi for the Quarter Ending 31 March 1843

No. of voucher	Nature of Payment	To whom paid	Amount Dollars	Cents
1	Services	Charles Preuss	93	00
2	Services	Joseph Bougar	144	00
3	Services	Charles Preuss	93	00
4	Services	Charles Preuss	84	00
5	Sundries	P. Chouteau, Jr. & Co.	317	00
6	Sundries	P. Chouteau, Jr. & Co.	88	75
7	Postage	J. C. Frémont	1	00
8	Services	J. N. Nicollet	1040	00
			$1860	75[9]

1. Payment at Washington, D.C., for services as assistant, 1 Dec. to 31 Dec. 1842.
2. *Voyageur* on first expedition.
3. Payment at Washington, D.C., for services as assistant, 1 Jan. to 31 Jan. 1843.
4. Payment at Washington, D.C., for services as assistant, 1 Feb. to 28 Feb. 1843.
5. For purchases (such as a lodge skin, ten pack saddles, fifty lbs. of lead, rifle, and powder horn) and services (shoeing horses and repair of guns) made at Fort John on 16 and 18 July 1843.
6. For purchases made at Fort John on the Laramie on 1 and 2 Sept. 1842. Such items as buckskin pants were not permitted and the total had to be reduced to $48.50; yet a statement of "Differences" would indicate that only $28 was not allowed.
7. Postage paid at Washington, D.C., on letter containing public accounts received from Chouteau and Co. in St. Louis.
8. Payment at Baltimore, Md., for services, 1 Nov. 1842 to 10 March 1843.
9. Because of the suspension of items in voucher no. 6, the final total was $1,820.50, and is so shown in the endorsement.

Military and Geographical Surveys West of the Mississippi for the Second, Third, and Fourth Quarters of 1843, and First, Second, and Third Quarters of 1844

No. of voucher	Nature of Payment	To whom paid	Amount Dollars	Cents
*1	Daguerreotype apparatus	James R. Chilton	78	25
2	Preserved meats, &c	J.E. Flandin	22	31
*3	Daguerreotype apparatus	H. Chilton	68	16
*4	Astl. Instruments &c.	Frye & Shaw	327	50
*5	India Rubber Boat &c.	Horace H. Day	302	10
6	Instruments	Arthur Stewart	215	00
*7	Outfit	Charles Renard	40	00
*8	do	J. & B. Bruce	115	00
9	do	Emory Low	5	63
10	Freight	Steamer Valley Forge	5	00
11	Horses	Louis Lajoie	120	00
12	do	Cyprian Billieau	65	00
13	do	John T. Pigott	110	00
†14	do	Louis Ménard	35	00
15	do	A. Sloan	45	00
16	Provisions	N. Berthoud	47	25
17	Printing blanks	S. Penn, Jr.	10	00
†18	Horse	Auguste Vasquez	25	00
19	do	Wm. G. Sholfield	35	00
20	do	Ewd. Ploudre	35	00
21	Mules	David Goodfellow	90	00
22	Horses	Archibald Sloan	55	00
23	do	A. Gallatin Boone	60	00
*24	Outfit	S.V. Farnsworth & Co.	66	44
25	Horse	George K. McGunegle	20	00
26	Outfit	A. Meier & Co.	52	15
27	do	Jacob Voglesang	6	00
*28	do	J.S. Mathews	2	50
29	do	T. Salorgue	20	00
30	Forage	B.W. Alexander	21	35
*31	Outfit	Edwd. Perry & Co.	172	37
32	Repairing arms	J. & S. Hawken	13	50
33	Stationary	S.W. Meech	28	20
34	Nails	James Conway	6	00
*35	Arms	Wm. Campbell	40	00
*36	Saddles, Bridles, Harnesses & c.	Thornton Grimsley	438	62
*37	Harness	Ross & Cowe	32	00
38	Equipment	G.W. Rogers	5	00
39	do	Joseph Cailloun	9	00
40	Provisions	N. Devillers & Co.	10	44
41	do	R.O. Taylor	17	78
*42	Making Tents	Z. Prevaud	25	00
*43	Equipment	N. Tiernan	140	00
*44	do	Jos. Murphy	181	20
45	do	John Hobson	30	00
*46	Instruments & c.	Jacob Blattner	27	00
*47	Equipment	N. Phillips	25	00

Note: "Do" listed under Nature of Payment refers to "same as above"

No. of voucher	Nature of Payment	To whom paid	Amount Dollars	Cents
48	Horse hire and forage	R. Mc O'Blinis	72	52
49	Equipment	K. McKenzie		88
50	do	E.W. & G. Poore	3	00
51	Provisions	F. Leonard	12	07
52	Provisions	E. Sisson	30	94
53	Horse	Benjn. Watson	30	00
54	Mules	D.W. Griffith	70	00
55	do	Thos. Peery	40	00
56	do	Mark R.C. Pulliam	35	00
57	Transportation, provisions, & c.	Steamer Col. Woods	150	42
58	Mules	Talton Turner	225	00
59	do	James Foster	25	00
60	do	Lucien Stewart	50	00
61	do	George Wilson	35	00
62	do	Phineas C. Islue	22	50
63	do	A.B.H. Magee	30	00
64	do	F.P. McGee	35	00
65	Repairs & c.	Gabriel Philibert	8	25
66	Horse	Luther M. Carter	40	00
67	Mules	L.D.W. Shaw	205	00
68	do	James M. Weathers	42	50
69	Horse	B. McDermott	25	00
70	Mules	Campbell & Sublette	160	00
71	do	Nathl. Bowman	30	00
72	Horse	Jas. T. Greenfield	26	00
73	Mule	Jas. M. Owen	40	00
74	Forage	Francis Bradley	16	55
75	Mule	S. Wade	25	00
76	Sundries	Boone & Hamilton	184	26
77	Mule	Jas. M. Simpson	40	00
78	Services	Oscar Sarpy	66	00
79	Provisions & c.	J. & E. Walsh	396	63
*†80	Mules & c.	Alex. Godey	200	00
81	Services	Ranson Clark	36	90
82	do	Jas. Power	36	00
83	do	Thos. Rogers	40	26
84	do	Jas. Rogers	40	26
*85	Lodge & poles	A.C. Metcalf	30	00
86	Mules, camp equipment &c.	Bent & St. Vrain & Co.	667	62
87	Services	Louis Menard	328	66
88	do	August Vasquez	90	90
89	do	François Lajeunesse	126	35
90	do	John Campbell	90	90
91	do	Clinton DeForrest	90	90
92	do	Michael Creely	90	90
93	do	Basil Lajeunesse	164	12
94	do	Alexis Parraw	90	90
95	do	Baptiste Tissant (Tesson)	90	90
96	do	Patrick White	90	90
97	do	Henry Lee	90	90
98	do	William Creuss	90	90
99	Provisions &c.	Hudson Bay Compy.	2038	65
100	Services	John G. Campbell	94	00
101	Provisions & c.	H.B. Brewer	267	89
102	Services	Philibert Cortot	122	65
103	do	Thos. Fallon	129	35
104	do	Jos. Verrot	211	50
105	do	Oliver Beaulieu	122	65
106	(Incompleted entry scratched)			

Note: "Do" listed under Nature of Payment refers to "same as above"

No. of voucher	Nature of Payment	To whom paid	Amount	
			Dollars	Cents
107	Mules & horses	John A. Sutter	2910	00
108	Sundries	John A. Sutter	981	93
109	do	C.W. Flügge	237	25
110	Provisions	Jos. B. Chiles	54	00
111	Services	Saml. Neal	211	00
112	Horses	Archibald Sloan	60	00
†113	do	Baptiste Derosier	18	00
114	Repairing Instruments	Jaccard & Co.	12	00
115	Horse shoes	Milton E. McGee	5	00
116	Mules	W.W. Gett	45	00
117	Services	Francis Parraw	179	10
118	Sundries	A. Robidoux	86	00
119	Services	Chas. Town	342	00
120	do	Christopher Carson	885	00
†121	Mules & Horse	Christopher Carson	140	00
122	Services	Louis Anderson	155	00
123	do	J.R. Walker	165	00
124	Sundries	Bent, St. Vrain & Co.	251	00
125	Provisions	E.T. Peery	37	00
126	Transportation of men	Steamboat Iatan	130	00
127	Services	Thomas Cowie	64	00
128	do	Louis Gouin Admr.	167	85
129	do	Saml. H. Davis	37	00
130	Repg. Instruments	C.D. Sullivan & Co.	4	00
131	Transportation	Chas. Preuss	216	80
132	Services	Jacob Dodson	493	00
133	Transportation	J.C. Frémont	216	80
134	Services	Jacob Dodson	493	00
†135	Horses	Wm. Perkins	80	00
136	Services	Wm. Perkins	239	16
137	Services	Louis Montreuil	221	85
138	do	Andres Fuentes	107	50
139	do	Thos. Fitzpatrick	1750	00
140	do	Alex (Ayot)	328	66
141	do	Tiery Wright	410	83
142	do	Raphael Proue	410	83
†143	do & provisions	Alexis Godare	918	00
144	do	Louis Zindel	573	52
†145	Transportation & c.	Thos. Fitzpatrick	309	50
146	Services	C. Taplin	410	83
147	do	Baptiste Bernier	493	00
148	do	Auguste Archambeau (lt)	190	00
149	(Entry scratched)			
150	(Entry scratched)			
151	Sundries	Robert Campbell	5455	35
152	Stationary	Wm. Fischer	26	39
153	Sundries	Chas. Preuss	38	40
			33092	38
154	Services	Theodore Talbot	986	00
			34078	38
155	do	Admr. Francois Badeau Sept. 19, 1844	387	00
			34465	38

J.C. Frémont
2nd. Lt. Topl. Engr.

Note: "Do" listed under Nature of Payment refers to "same as above"

MILEAGE TABLES
ALONG
THE ROAD TRAVELLED BY THE EXPEDITION IN 1843 AND 1844

OUTWARD JOURNEY

From Kansas Landing to Fort Vancouver

Date	Distance travelled each day	Distance from Kansas Landing	Localities
1843	*Miles*	*Miles*	
May 29	7	7	
June 8	5	187	Junction of Smoky Hill and Republican Forks, *Kansas*
25	26	516	Crossing of the Republican, *Colorado*
30	26	644	South Fork of the Platte River, *Colorado*
July 4	18	751	St. Vrain's Fort (*traveled 300 miles to Pueblo and returned*), Colo.
Aug. 2	31	918	Medicine Bow River, *Wyoming*
4	18	962	North Fork Platte River, *Wyoming*
9	26	1,066	Sweetwater River, *Wyoming*
13	24	1,167	South Pass, *Continental Divide, Wyoming*
15	29	1,221	Green River,*Wyoming*
25	8	1,463	Beer Springs, *Idaho*
Sept. 3	3	1,636	Mouth of Bear River, *Utah*
8	20	1,714	Shore of Salt Lake, *Utah*
9	8	1,722	Island in the Salt Lake, *Utah*
18	23	1,906	Fort Hall, *Idaho (remained 4 days)*
24	10	1,928	American Falls on Lewis Fork, *Idaho*
Oct. 10	2	2,256	Fort Boise, *Idaho*
26	3	2,518	Fort Nez Perce, at the Mouth of Walahalah River, (*Walla Walla*), *Washington*
Nov. 4	14	2,676	The Dalles, *Washington*
6&7	90	2,766	Fort Vancouver, *Washington*

The above were calculations taken by the Fremont Party
and entered by Fremont in his journal. Italics represent
the present day location of the Fremont campsites.

MILEAGE TABLES
ALONG
THE ROAD TRAVELLED BY THE EXPEDITION IN 1843 AND 1844

HOMEWARD JOURNEY

From The Dalles to the Missouri River

Date		Distance travelled each day	Distance from The Dalles	Localities
1843		*Miles*	*Miles*	
Nov.	25	12	12	
Dec.	10	15	250	Tlamath Lake, *(Klamath Lake), Oregon*
	16	9	318	Summer Lake, *Oregon*
	20	26	391	Lake Abert, *Oregon*
	24	13	446	Christmas Lake, *Oregon*
Jan.	6	15	647	Great Boiling Spring, *(Double Hot Springs), Nevada*
	12	6	684	Pyramid Lake, *Nevada*
	16	18	735	*Truckee River, Nevada*
	17	22	757	*Carson River, Nevada*
	20	5	788	*Near Fort Churchill, Nevada*
	22	14	826	*Smith Valley, Nevada*
	23	25	851	*South west of Hawthorne, Nevada*
	24	20	871	*Vicinity of Aurora, Nevada*
	25	25	896	*Bridgeport, California (remained 2 days)*
	27	12	908	*Swauger Creek, California*
	28	12	920	*Mount 8422, (Mt. Lewis), California*
	29	7	927	*Split party: Fremont ,near Coleville , California*
				Cannon party at mouth of the West Walker River Canyon
	30	11	938	*Long Valley, California*
	31	26	964	*Markleville, California*
Feb.	2	16	980	*Grover's Hot Springs, California*
	20	3	1,001	Summit of the Sierra Nevada, *Carson Pass, California*
March	6	34	1,142	Nueva Helvetia, *(Sacramento), California*
April	13	27	1,559	Summit of the Sierra, *(Tehachapi Pass), California*
	20	33	1,713	Spanish Trail at Mohavve, *(Mohave River), California*
May	6	18	2,005	Rio Virgen *(Virgin River), Utah*
	12	14	2,084	Vegas de Santa Clara, *Utah*
	23	12	2,269	Sevier River, *Utah*
	26	9	2,333	Utah Lake, *Utah*
June	3	21	2,497	Uintah Fort, *Utah*
	7	30	2,568	Green River (Brown's Hole), *Utah*
	15	25	2,764	New Park, *Colorado*
	17	33	2,823	Old Park, *Colorado*
	22	15	2,913	Bayou Salade (South Park), *Colorado*
July	29	30	3,063	Pueblo, on the Arkansas, *Pueblo, Colorado*
	1	33	3,133	Bent's Fort, *Colorado*
	8	28	3,243	Head water of Smoky Hill fork of the Kansas, *Kansas*
Aug.	31	8	3,702	Kansas Landing, *(Kansas City), Missouri*
	1	7	3,709	Missouri River, *Missouri*

The above were calculations taken by the Fremont Party and entered by Fremont in his journal. Italics represent the present day location of the Fremont campsites.

Table of Latitudes and Longitudes Deduced
from the Annexed Observations

Date		Latitudes	Longitudes	Localities
1843				
Dec.	13	121° 20' 42"	121° 20' 42"	Tributary to the lake and head water of the Tlamath river
	24	42 23 25	---	Christmas Lake
	31	41 19 55	---	New Years Camp
1844				
Jan.	3	40 48 15	---	Camp near the Mud Lake
	6	40 39 46	---	Camp near Great Boiling Spring (*Double Hot Springs*)
	15	39 51 13	---	Pyramid Lake, mouth of Salmon Trout River (*Truckee River*)
	18	39 24 16	---	Camp on the river of the Sierra Nevada (*Carson River*)
	19	39 19 21	---	Camp on the river of the Sierra Nevada (*Carson River*)
	21	39 03 53	---	Camp on the river of the Sierra Nevada
	22	38 49 54	---	Camp on a river, near a gap
	23	38 36 19	---	Camp on a southern branch of a stream of encampment of 22nd & 23rd.
	24	38 24 28	---	Head waters of a stream
	26	38 18 01	---	Camp on a large stream (*East Walker River*)
	30	38 37 18	---	Camp on the same stream which we encamped upon on the night of the 18th & 19th of January (*Carson River*)
Feb.	5	38 42 26	---	First camp in the pass of the Sierra Nevada
	14,19	38 41 57	120 25 57	The long camp
	24	38 46 58	120 34 20	Rio de los Americanos, (*High in the mountains*)
Mar.	10,22	38 34 42	---	Nueva Helvetia (*Sacramento*)
	25	38 08 23	121 23 03	Rio de los Mukelemnes (*Mokelumne River*)
	26	38 02 48	121 16 22	Rio de los Mukelemnes
	28	37 42 26	121 07 13	Stanislaus River
	31	37 15 43	120 46 30	Stanislaus River
	3	37 22 05	120 58 03	Large tributary of the San Joaquin, (no name)
April	4	37 08 00	120 45 22	San Joaquin River
	5	36 49 12	120 28 34	San Joaquin River
	8	36 24 50	119 41 40	Lake fork, (of the Tulares)
	9	36 08 38	119 22 02	Small stream affluent to the lake (Tulares)
	10	35 49 10	118 56 34	Small stream affluent to the lake (Tulares)
	13	35 17 12	118 35 03	Near pass creek in the mountains, (Sierra Nevada)
	14	35 03 00	118 18 09	Small stream east of the Sierra Nevada
	15	34 41 42	118 20 00	Rock spring
	18	34 27 03	117 43 21	Spring heads of a stream among foot hills of a mountain
	21	34 34 11	117 13 00	Mohahve River, on the Spanish trail from Pueblo de los Angeles to Santa Fe
	24	35 03 00	116 29 19	Mohahve River, on the Spanish trail from Pueblo de los Angeles to Santa Fe
	25	35 13 08	116 23 28	Aqua de Tomaso, on the Spanish trail
	29	35 51 21	---	Hernandez spring
May	1	35 58 19	---	Deep spring hole on a river which loses itself in the sands
	3	36 10 20	---	Las Vegas, Nevada

The above were calculations taken by the Fremont Party and entered by Fremont in his journal. Italics represent the present day location of the Fremont campsites.